The Book of Stupidity: a context on stupidity and conscience

The Book of Stupidity: a context on stupidity and conscience
Michael Sousa

© Michael Sousa
The Book of Stupidity: a context on stupidity and conscience

"All rights reserved. Except as otherwise provided by law, it is not permitted to reproduce this work in whole or in part, nor to incorporate it into a computer system, nor to transmit it in any form or by any means (electronic, mechanical, photocopying, recording or others) without the prior written permission of the copyright holders. Infringement of such rights entails legal sanctions and may constitute an offence against intellectual property."

"There is no sin except stupidity" – Oscar Wilde

Summary

- **Part 1 - Stupidity**

1. Prologue: Good, Bad or... Stupid?.................................07
2. Are we all stupid? The Three Narcissistic Wounds................. 10
3. Defining Stupidity: The Dunning-Kruger Effect....................13
4. Peter's Principle or How to Deal with a Stupid Boss......... 20
5. The Fourth Estate: When Stupid Inform Others Stupid..........27
6. The Anekdoty: The Jokes That Could Kill You..................... 31
7. Modern Geopolitics: The "Inevitable" Nuclear Stupidity.....36
8. A Tale: Justice and Stupidity......................................46
9. Noticing Stupidity: The Power of the Word........................ 54
10. A Hope Against Stupidity: Education.............................. 77
11. Epilogue: Dealing with a Black Swan.............................81

- **Part 2 – Neurosis**

0. Prologue: Neurosis... What does it consist of?...................... 89
1. Chapter 1: The Origin of Psychoanalysis 94
2. Chapter 2: Defining Neurosis......................................100
3. Chapter 3: Psychoanalytic Concepts Related to Neurosis........... 105
4. Chapter 4: Anxiety Neurosis 111
5. Chapter 5: Obsessive-Compulsive Neurosis. 117
6. Chapter 6: Hysteria..124
7. Chapter 7: Phobias and Phobic Neuroses 130
8. Chapter 8: Defense Mechanisms and Neurosis 139
9. Chapter 9: Psychosexual Development and Neurosis....... 148
10. Chapter 10: Transference and Countertransference 152
11. Chapter 11: Freud's Classical Case Analysis 159
12. Chapter 12: Modern Approaches in the Therapy of Neuroses.166
13. Epilogue: The Future of Psychoanalysis............................171

- **Part 3 – Consciousness**

0. Prologue: Are we all conscious?.. 179
1. Chapter 1: What is Consciousness?... 193
2. Chapter 2: Consciousness in the Evolutionary Context.........199
3. Chapter 3: Consciousness and the Bicameral Theory……...205
4. Chapter 4: Neuroscience of Consciousness............................ 212
5. Chapter 5: Consciousness and Altered States …......…..…... 219
6. Chapter 6: Artificial Intelligence and Consciousness..............227
7. Chapter 7: Consciousness in Contemporary Philosophy…….235
8. Chapter 8: Neuroplasticity and the Shaping of Consc.…...... 243
9. Chapter 9: The Unconscious …………………………….... 251
10. Chapter 10: Consciousness in Altered States….....…….......260
11. Chapter 11: Conscience and Free Will……......................268
12. Chapter 12: The Future of Consciousness: ……….……...274
13. Chapter 13: Consciousness and Spirituality...........................281
14. Epilogue: The Journey of Self-Awareness ………....….…..288

Prologue
Good, bad or... stupid?

We're all stupid. To a greater or lesser extent, with a greater or lesser harmful impact on ourselves and society.
"Never attribute to wickedness what can be adequately explained by stupidity." This is Hanlon's Razor, an epigram that tries to demonstrate that, many times, bad actions, acts or events that could be linked to villainy and evil are nothing more than consequences of the most beautiful and simple stupidity.

The concepts of good and evil and their complexity have afflicted man and influenced his psyche for eons. The ancient religions, especially those that most influenced the development of the Western world and its culture, are almost always Manichean, almost never having a middle ground between right and wrong, always with absolute measures in relation to the subjects treated. Of course, in the modern world society has adapted to these concepts, learning that a truth is never absolute and that understanding right and wrong, 'good and evil', is actually a much more complex and difficult task (do you really get it?).

Going back to the premise that mistakes, cruel acts, and historically bad decisions are driven more by stupidity than by evil, before examples let's look at some concepts about what stupidity actually is and how it moves and influences human decisions and interactions.

A stupid person is a person who causes harm to another person or group of people, without, at the same time, obtaining any advantage for himself or even suffering a loss, a definition by the Italian historian Carlo Cipolla, which we will delve into in the course of the next chapters.

In this regard, nature seems to have really outdone itself. The extraordinary thing about stupidity is its ubiquity, that is, everything and everyone is subject to its power, all the time, everywhere. Either by our own actions or, especially, by others.

It is not difficult to understand how political, economic, or bureaucratic power amplifies the harmful potential of a stupid person. But we must still understand what makes a stupid person so dangerous; in other words, what does the power of stupidity consist in.

Essentially, stupid people are dangerous because sensible people find it difficult to imagine or understand their behavior. An intelligent person can understand the logic of a crook. The bandit's actions follow a model of rationality, perverse but still rational. The bad guy wants something you own. Theft is not just, but it is rational, and if it is rational, it can be calculated, predicted. One can, in short, predict the actions of a bandit, his maneuvers and thus prepare for it.

With a stupid person, all this becomes very difficult. Apparently irrational actions based on totally erroneous or even random interpretations of some concept or idea, or even instinct, that someone more sensible would understand without much regret, ends up being very difficult to decipher when using rationality to interpret a decision that, most of the time, did not have the slightest logical basis to be made.

Empathy in the face of dictators or ideologies linked to them, or even inaction in the face of actions that endanger one's own freedom or that of others, is also an act of stupidity.

There is no rational method for predicting whether, when, how, where, or why a stupid creature will carry out its decisions.

Therefore, when faced with a stupid individual, we always run the risk of being at his mercy. However, we cannot credit or classify their actions as necessarily good or bad, or even purposeful, only as actions, in a context that we will rarely fully understand.

What remains for us not to be so at the mercy (of what is in us and what is in others), is to understand a little better stupidity, its bases, its nuances, what it is and how it impacts our lives.

Are we all stupid? Humanity's Three Narcissistic Wounds

"The Self is not master in its own abode" – Sigmund Freud

The father of psychoanalysis, Sigmund Freud, articulated a concept that challenged the notion of humanity's superiority and centrality in the universe. He called this concept "The Three Narcissistic Wounds of Humanity." These wounds represent historical moments in which the collective self-esteem of humanity, in its conception, was profoundly shaken. Each of these wounds challenged our view of ourselves and our place in the cosmos.

The First Wound: The Copernican Revolution

For most of history, mankind has firmly believed in the geocentric view of the universe, where the Earth was at the center and everything revolved around it. This concept has been widely accepted and reinforced by philosophy and theology. Nicolaus Copernicus, however, proposed a radically different view in the 16th century. He suggested that the Earth was not the center of the universe, but that it orbited the Sun, along with other planets.

This paradigm shift was a deep narcissistic wound. Humanity had to confront the idea that it was not the center of the universe, but only a part of a vast, indifferent solar system. This revelation shook humanity's confidence in its cosmic importance and ushered in a new era of scientific thought.

The Second Wound: Darwin's Theory of Evolution

The second wound came with Charles Darwin in the nineteenth century, with his theory of evolution by natural selection. Until then, the prevailing view was that human beings were divine creations, distinct from and superior to all other living beings. Darwin, however, showed that all species, including humans, evolved from common ancestors through natural processes.

This revelation was a direct blow to human pride. Discovering that we are part of the tree of life, sharing ancestors with other life forms, was a deep wound in the realization of our own uniqueness and superiority. Darwin's theory not only challenged the religious beliefs of the time, but also reconfigured humanity's understanding of its own origin and place in the natural world.

The Third Wound: The Freudian Unconscious

The third narcissistic wound was inflicted by Sigmund Freud himself in the early 20th century. Freud, however, introduced the concept of the unconscious, arguing that much of our behavior is influenced by unconscious desires and fears, which are beyond conscious control.

This idea was a severe blow to the human ego. The notion that we are not fully masters of our own minds, and that unconscious forces shape our behavior, was a disturbing revelation. Freud demonstrated that the human mind is more complex and less controllable than previously imagined, challenging the view that we are purely rational beings.

Freud's three narcissistic wounds represent critical moments in the history of human thought in which our view of ourselves has been radically challenged. Each of these wounds has forced us to reconsider our position in the universe, our origin, and the nature of our own mind.

These challenges, while painful, have been fundamental to the progress of human knowledge. They taught us to embrace the complexity of the cosmos, the beauty of evolution, and the depth of the human mind. By confronting these hard truths, humanity has become more aware of its true condition and better able to explore the vast frontiers of knowledge.

But if we are not at the center of the Universe, if we are not divine creatures, and if we have no real control over our actions and decisions, if we are dominated by the unconscious that we do not see or understand, can we only be stupid?

Defining Stupidity:
The Dunning-Kruger Effect and Human Stupidity

To better understand the reality of the world in which we live, we should, first of all, better understand the behavior of its main factor of change: the individual. And so, from the individual, we could better understand the behavior of his group.

When we analyze the individual, or their group, we look for a pattern that has led them to a situation that is not pleasant or ideal. That is, when the situation is bad, we analyze the history in an attempt to understand how we got there, what were the behaviors, decisions, and interpretations that led them to that moment. When we talk about a group, it can be a family, a company, a country or humanity itself.

Studying the paths traced, the history, we observe the errors of decisions, misinterpretations, completely wrong or poorly founded conclusions. And, regarding these paths and interpretations that lead us to a bad reality or with unpleasant consequences, one can find several failures of management, interpretation or even access to information, but what prevails in relation to all these factors, and even causes them, is a single and indispensable one, stupidity.

To better understand stupidity, let's briefly look at its five fundamental laws, masterfully described by the Italian economist and historian Carlo Cipolla in The Basic Laws of Human Stupidity (Allegro Ma Non Troppo) (1988).

The Fundamental Laws of Human Stupidity (Le leggi fondamentali della stupidità umana)

First, in this chapter of the book, Cipolla classifies humanity into four groups:

- The intelligent ones, who manage to have an action that results in an advantage for themselves and for society;

- Swindlers, who take advantage of themselves to the detriment of others, or of society;

- The naïve, who generate advantage to others, causing harm to themselves;

- The stupid ones, who have an action that results in harm to themselves and others.

(We could here make a superficial parallel to the clinical structures of psychoanalysis)
After that, the author enunciates the five laws of stupidity, which define his behavior in society:

1. Always and inevitably, each of us underestimates the number of stupid individuals in the world.

2. The probability that a given person is stupid is independent of any other characteristic of himself.

3. A person is stupid if he causes harm to another or to a group without gaining any benefit for himself, or even suffering harm. (Golden Law)

4. Non-stupid people always underestimate the harmful potential of stupid people; They constantly forget that at any time and place, and under any circumstance, dealing with or associating with stupid individuals is inevitably a costly mistake.

5. The stupid person is the most dangerous kind of person there is.

In common sense we have the concept of the chess pigeon complex, which could be a synthesis of these laws. This term appeared on the internet to summarize stupid attitudes (non-theoretically based arguments, fallacies, etc.), in discussions or debates:

"Arguing with 'so-and-so' is like playing chess with a pigeon: he defecates on the board, knocks over the pieces, and flies off singing victory."

The stupid individual's movements and their consequences are based on his arrogance and confidence, whether to act, make decisions or even the completely questionable certainties he possesses about his own knowledge and reasoning.

Noting this, excusing Asimov (and Carlo Cipolla himself), we can add here the Zero Law of human stupidity and all its evils:

The Dunning-Kruger Effect

The Dunning-Kruger effect implies a phenomenon where individuals who have little or no knowledge about a topic believe they know more about that subject than others, or even more than authorities and experts on the subject.
This confidence makes them not have a real perception of the problem or the situation, thus leading them to bad, often catastrophic results, even more so when these individuals are in positions and positions that make their illusion have consequences for a larger group or for society as a whole.

We see here at work the stupid of Cipolla's definition, the one who manages to cause harm to himself and others by his lack of perception or understanding of reality, but who blindly believes that he has this understanding. In social psychology, this overestimation of one's own qualities and abilities is recognized as illusory superiority.

This mechanism of illusory superiority was demonstrated by Justin Kruger and David Dunning at Cornell University. In the study, published in the Journal of Personality and Social Psychology in 1999, the researchers found that in a variety of skills, even different ones, from reading comprehension and interpretation, to driving, to playing chess or tennis, ignorance and lack of real perception of one's own abilities generates confidence more intensely and more often than actually having knowledge or experience in the subject.

Dunning and Kruger therefore proposed patterns of behavior that stupid people will incur in certain situations:

- Failing to recognize your own lack of ability;

- Failing to recognize the genuine abilities in other people;

- Failing to recognize the extent of one's own incompetence and stupidity;

- But they can recognize and admit their own lack of skill after they have been trained for that skill.

Dunning draws an analogy as if this effect were a pathological condition, a physical disability, but the individual does not perceive it, or even denies its existence, even in cases where this disability is evident to everyone else and incapacitates him from performing the most ordinary activities.

"When people are incompetent in the strategies they adopt to achieve success and satisfaction, they suffer a double burden: not only do they come to erroneous conclusions and make unfortunate choices, but their incompetence robs them of the ability to realize it. Instead, they get the wrong impression that they're doing very well."

It's that famous joke: "When you die, you don't know you're dead. It's just painful and hard for others. The same applies when you're stupid."

"If you're incompetent, you can't know you're incompetent ... [T]he skills needed to provide a correct answer are exactly the skills you need to have to be able to recognize what a correct answer is. In logical reasoning, in child-rearing, in administration, in problem-solving, the skills you use to get the correct answer are exactly the same skills you use to evaluate the answer. Therefore, we have continued investigations to find out if the same conclusion could be true in other areas. And to our surprise, it was very true."

– Words of David Dunning in an interview with The New York Times in 2010.

Dunning and Kruger tested their hypotheses with Cornell University students enrolled in psychology courses, giving them assessments, mainly logic and grammar. After receiving their test scores, the researchers asked the participants to estimate their level of skill with the topics in relation to the other participants. The group most competent in each skill correctly estimated their own level, while the incompetent group overestimated it.

Meanwhile, people with real knowledge tended to underestimate their competence. Basically, those who considered the tasks easy assumed that the tasks were also easy for the other participants.

When we understand all these patterns, we recognize stupid individuals and their effects on society, whether through the consequences and evils they cause to themselves or to everyone. We realize how harmful and dangerous the risk of stupid individuals in positions of power and leadership can be, and how much we should not submit to any kind of authority, real or not.

The course of history has often been altered, or atrocities have been committed, simply because there was too much authority in the hands of too few idiots. Any resemblance to historical or current politics is no coincidence.
The stupid, perhaps, precisely because of a wrong perception of reality and their own incapacity, are able to guide the most important decisions in a society by their hubris and excess of self-confidence. And it definitely shouldn't be that way.

As Bertrand Russell put it: "The trouble of the world is that intelligent people are full of doubts, and idiotic people are full of certainties."

Stupidity at Work: Peter's Principle or How to Deal with a Stupid Boss

Let's address some aspects of our lives where stupidity can have a greater impact. I believe that common to all mortals, the work environment stands out for the amount of stupid people one can meet.

The Peter Principle, or The Principle of Incompetence, was presented by the psychologist and structuralist theorist Laurence J. Peter, in his work "The Peter Principle", published in 1969 in the United States, having reached the general public years later and remaining on the New York Times bestseller list for more than a year, in addition to still being printed today, more than 50 years after its launch. Below we have the maxim of the Peter Principle:

"In a hierarchical system, every employee tends to be promoted to his or her level of incompetence."

In his book, Peter presents several terms and descriptions to recognize an incompetent who fits the principle:

- The hypersimophobia complex (the latent fear felt by superiors when a subordinate shows strong managerial and competence potential);

- Oscillation syndrome (inability or fear to make decisions, avoiding situations in which changes and decisions are important in their management);

- Laughter inertia (habit of telling jokes instead of working, or even making jokes with others, as a way of reaffirming one's "competence") or

- Tabulating gigantism (obsession with being more competent than one's peers, worthy of more recognition and, again, excessive self-assertion).

I'm sure that the reader, while reading the descriptions, remembered some manager with whom he has had (or still has) contact. The one who writes to you (who has been a manager and an analyst) can think of some that fit perfectly.

Due to the complex of hypersimophobia and oscillation syndrome, there are managers who put themselves in comical situations, such as in the situation when a team arrived with a defined project, and the same asked for one or another change (almost always only an opinion), to demonstrate some kind of participation, or that their decision was somehow "fundamental" for the execution.

The team usually has to submit to this opinion, not to an in-depth or experienced analysis by a manager with knowledge or real desire to improve the project/product, and then make the changes to something that was technically good, perhaps making it not so good, simply because of a lack of knowledge and the need to assert oneself as a manager.

This complete certainty of knowing how things work (even if you don't have the knowledge to possess all that certainty), limits improvements and optimizations that other subordinates could bring you.

About the inertia of laughter and tabulating gigantism, it is usually about a manager who insists on making jokes and criticizing the decisions of other managers and his co-workers, with whom he is in contact all the time.

Or when he doesn't spend hours on end stating how much better he would do the work of other managers, always having a scathing critique for every decision he learned. All this pedantically self-assertive behavior is nothing more than the very realization of one's incompetence, looking for ways to deny it to oneself and others around one.

We can frame these situations and the incompetent manager in the Dunning-Kruger Effect, when an individual has complete confidence that he has knowledge in a certain topic (or even in management and leadership skills), but in reality is a complete inept in the subject.

Realizing this, we realize how harmful these incompetent managers are, not only to their subordinates or their teams, but to companies as a whole. Managers who manage areas and do not have the knowledge for management, because they have stagnated in time and position and have become completely stupid for the role. We can fit them into some definitions of stupidity brought by Carlo Cipolla, in this case, specifically the 4th Law of Stupidity:

"Non-stupid people always underestimate the harmful potential of stupid people; they constantly forget that at any time and place, and under any circumstance, dealing with or associating with stupid individuals is inevitably a costly mistake." – Carlo Cipolla's 4th Law of Stupidity.

Such managers and leaders have stopped learning, either because they do not seek more knowledge in specializations and leadership itself, or even within the company's own processes, because they think that they have already learned everything, because they have reached such a position in an organization.

A management deficiency that can be treated by the disabled professional and, mainly, by the people and talent management area, responsible for the monitoring and development of this professional.

In the papper "Promotions and the Peter Principle" by Danielle Li and Kelly Shue, the economists and researchers stated that those who became managers simply because they performed better in middle positions were about 6 percent worse than their previous bosses, that is, they reduced the performance of all their subordinates by about 6 percent.

It is thought that an individual in a middle position, because he has had some outstanding performance, deserves promotion, when in fact he may not have the necessary attributes for leadership or even basic characteristics of interpersonal intelligence.

Managers like this make companies less efficient, and the financial costs of this kind of incompetent management are difficult to calculate. Modern corporations have tried to better understand these failures and how much they lose by putting unfit individuals in leadership positions, who cause more bureaucracy and problems, rather than diminish them, and undermine the development of competent ideas and teams.

In another very interesting study on the Peter Principle, James Ike Schaap, Ph.D. and adjunct professor at the University of Nevada in the United States, states that these superiors in their levels of incompetence will always seek to keep subordinates within bureaucratic, limiting values and about their ignorance, that is, they will be more formalistic and demanding the fulfillment of inefficient methods established by them. And they will try to fit each subordinate into this pattern, altering the team, through hiring and firing, so that it increasingly fits into their own incompetences.

These managers, in addition to making the company less efficient and less profitable, also hinder the development of their subordinates and their own careers, because if they leave the position, they will prove to be completely outdated and backward for a constant and evolving market.

We see, therefore, the incompetent manager fit even more into the standards of stupidity defined by Carlo Cipolla, as we can see in the Golden Law's definition of human stupidity:

"A person is stupid if he causes harm to another or to a group without obtaining any benefit for himself, or even suffering harm." – Carlo Cipolla's 3rd Law of Stupidity.

By Peter's principle it is understood that someone can join a company as an intern; From this beginning, he may move on, by merit, to some position of effective technical level; From there he would rise to new positions until, for example, a manager, where he would reveal himself to be a complete incompetent.

With this, his ascension would end and this person would be stagnant in a function for which he has no competence to exercise.

Therefore, no matter what technical knowledge and insights the subordinate possesses, these incompetent managers often have no insight into what is really going on in their own sectors or even know what the attributes or capabilities of their employees are, much less how to use this for team development and problem solving.

These managers waste more time trying to assert themselves and justify the position instead of properly managing it, of taking charge of the development of the people on their team, the primary function of a leader.

And what do you do when you come across such a manager in front of you? Unfortunately there isn't much. An incompetent manager who stays in office for a long time is only an indicator of the structural and hierarchical failure in the organization.

An organization that has not yet realized the damage (in terms of human and financial capital) of remaining an incompetent manager tends not to notice talents or solve a problem like this in the short term. Sometimes, competent people can only look for a place where incompetence is not a valued trait.

The Fourth Estate: When Stupid Inform Other Stupid

"Eu não preciso ler jornais, mentir sozinho eu sou capaz" – Cowboy fora da lei – Raul Seixas

When thinking about the power of the media and newspapers, it is impossible not to remember Charles Foster Kane, the press magnate and character in Orson Welles' masterpiece, Citizen Kane, a character who owns several newspapers, in which he writes what he wants, distorting the truth and the facts, according to his own opinion and will.

Fourth Estate is a term commonly used to describe how journalism and the media can exert a powerful influence on society. The term is so named in reference to the Three Powers existing in a Democratic State: the Legislative, the Executive and the Judiciary.

It is generally used to describe how the press acts in society through news and entertainment of all kinds and that are brought to the general public (today, in various ways and possible means), with topics ranging from politics, elections, important debates for society, events, discoveries and innovations, fashion and health.

Therefore, the de facto power of the media at various levels is undeniable, and its definition as a "fourth estate" is perhaps not so exaggerated. The use of the media by despots and totalitarian regimes as a means of propaganda and manipulation is classic, but in regimes such as these the media becomes only an extension of the will and opinion of the state.

It is elementary that the attempt of any State to limit in some way or "regulate" the media is to give only one more power to one of the Powers, making uncertain any type of communication, news and any information that may come to the population and that involves the State and its members. Definitely, this path is one that leads us to authoritarianism, untruths and stupidity.

We have thus shown how freedom and democracy are intimately linked to journalism, the media and freedom of the press. For the Frenchman Alexis de Tocqueville and the American Thomas Jefferson, the freedom of the people and the freedom of the press are like a single freedom, where there is simply no democracy if there is no truly free press.

The famous First Amendment to the U.S. Constitution, which was adopted in 1791, briefly prevents the U.S. government from infringing on six fundamental rights, such as:

Establish an official religion or give preference to a particular religion (establishes the separation of Church and State);
Prohibit the free exercise of religion;
Limit freedom of expression;
Limit freedom of the press;
Limit the right to peaceful free association;
Limit the right to petition the government for redress.
In solid democracies, the slightest kind of interference by the state in the media or the media is not even imagined.

There are several studies and academic research on how the influence of the mainstream media can affect social decisions, public opinion, what and how news reaches the population and how this can define their direction. And about "defining the direction of society", we can talk about everything from who will be the president of a nation, what proposals should be discussed in a parliament, to what kind of car you should drive, what to wear or what to eat for breakfast.

Defining this, we realize that we do not know very well the extent of this power in a democracy with freedom of the press (as said, there is no one without the other) and what kinds of risks the abuse of this power by those who hold it can negatively influence society and the lives of individuals.

During the bloody and necessary French Revolution, Jean-Paul Marat, in addition to being one of the most prominent and influential figures of the Revolution, owned the newspaper L'Ami du peuple (The Friend of the People), a newspaper where he imposed his persistent persecution and declarations of hatred on the more moderate groups, actions that made him fall into the graces of the people and, thus, making his newspaper one of the leading sources of news at the time.

Through his newspaper he persecuted not only the more moderate political group, but also personal enemies or even people with whom he had the slightest quarrel, accusing them of conspiracy against the revolution, inciting the fury of his readers and, in many cases, causing innocent people to be sentenced to the guillotine. About 40,000 people lost their lives on the guillotine without any kind of trial.

Marat was responsible for the creation and dissemination of the expression "enemy of the people", which had been adopted by the Soviet regime during Stalin's Great Purge, to classify people accused of anti-revolutionary activities and crimes against the state. Marat used to name the "enemies of the people" in his newspaper, inciting the populace and calling for their execution.

Marat's newspaper defined entire destinies and also important paths of the revolution guided by his simple will and opinion.

In an extreme situation like a revolution, we have a Fourth Estate despot who manipulate society and the destinies of a nation. In a stabilized democracy, we have this power exercised in nuances, not only at the political or ideological level, but in so many different aspects, themes, characteristics, and means that it is practically impossible to enumerate them all.

It is not up to the State to limit the scope of the Fourth Estate, which would undoubtedly only corrupt it in its own will. It is all up to the individual, perhaps, who should try to keep himself informed in the most impartial and comprehensive way possible, understanding facts, not opinions, not accepting the influences he does not want, trying to recognize these subtle movements (sometimes not so much) that the owners and exercisers of this power try to inflict on us.

A Bit of History
Anekdoty: The Jokes That Could Kill You

Regarding the stupid chaos that the recent conflicts between the West and Russia put humanity again at risk of nuclear war, it becomes inevitable not to remember the Cold War; their risks, fears, and how close humanity was to becoming extinct, in addition to the good jokes that could come up about living under an absurd regime:

'A delegation from Georgia visits Stalin. They go into your office, then they leave. As soon as they leave, the dictator starts looking for his pipe. It opens drawers, cabinets, and nothing. Then he shouts to the head of the secret police:
'I lost my pipe, go to the delegation and see if anyone has taken it.'
A few hours later, Stalin unwittingly finds his pipe in one of the drawers and shouts again to the head of the secret police:
'Alright, I found my pipe!'
'Too late,' replies the chief, entering the room.
"Half of the delegation confessed to catching it and the other half died during interrogation."

The anekdoty were jokes that the citizens of the countries under Soviet rule made about their own regime or situations that communism applied there put them through.

These jokes were most often passed on as discreetly as possible to each other in order to avoid reprisals from the Soviet Secret Police, which, considering the jokes as "Anti-Communist Propaganda", maintained censorship and absurd reprisals, hallmarks of communist regimes, on such expressions of political dissent.

In the USSR, a woman goes to a dealership to buy a car and the salesman says, "All right, in 10 years you can come and get your car." "In the morning or in the afternoon?" the woman asks. "What difference does it make?" the salesman asks. "The plumber comes in the morning," the woman replies.

The documentary Hammer & Tickle: The Communist Joke Book, made in 2006 by Ben Lewis, which traveled for two years to several countries of the former Iron Curtain to show the story of how jokes served as an outlet for the expression of the people about the desires for reform and freedom in their countries.

Everything has become manipulated by the state. There were more things to joke about because there was so much intervention, in everything. For humor to be worthy of state analysis was the fact that it encompassed all aspects of everyday life. From the purchase of bread to the decisions of the leaders, everything became a joke.

Stalin reads his report to the Party Congress. Suddenly, someone sneezes. "Who sneezed?" Silence. "The first line! Standing! Shoot!" They are shot, and he asks again, "Who sneezed, comrades?" No response. "Second row! Standing! Shoot!" And these are shot as well. "Well, who sneezed?" At last a sobbing cry resounds in the Congress hall, "It was me!" Stalin says: "Cheers, comrade!"

The state was everything. So jokes were told about everything. Citizens considered the jokes an act of rebellion against oppression and lack of freedom. The manipulation and commotion of humor was seen in such a powerful way that, according to Lewis, many people who lived in the Soviet bloc claimed that humor was what had really brought down communism.

For disseminating these jokes, countless people have been imprisoned or even sent to concentration camps.

The agency responsible for investigating and arresting the jokers was the Secret Service itself. The documentary states that there were periods when a significant number of people were convicted for the jokes. It is not yet known how many of these accusations were specifically about jokes, but it is possible to see how dangerous it was and how much it bothered the Communist Party.

We also have the famous trilemma attributed to the Slovenian philosopher Slavoj Žižek, although he cites him as having anonymous authorship, a "witty formula" for life under communism:

Of the three characteristics: 'personal honesty', 'sincere support for the regime' and 'intelligence' – it was possible to combine only two, never all three. When you were honest and participative, you weren't very bright; when you were brilliant and participative, you weren't honest; And if someone was honest and brilliant, they weren't participatory.

In Brazil, anti-communist jokes are also very famous. The most famous version that is around here is the well-known Russian Reversal.

Reversal Russa was created by Ukrainian comedian Yakov Smirnoff, who was born and raised when Ukraine was part of the Soviet Union and later moved to the United States.

In these jokes, the subject and direct object of the sentence are inverted, with comedic intent and criticism of the regime:

*"In America, you always find a party.
In the Soviet Union, the party always finds you.'*

Possibly the greatest propagator of anti-communism and Soviet Union jokes was not even born in Eastern Europe.

Ronald Reagan, one of the most important presidents of the United States, creator of the Reaganomics economic plan and author of the term "Evil Empire" to refer to the Soviet Union, was known for his good humor and his many jokes about communism at the end of his speeches.

There are stories that even Mikhail Gorbachev didn't miss out on hearing one of his jokes in person.

The jokes of the people in the USSR, however infamous, were for a long time the only way to keep the spirit of opposition and the yearning for freedom of expression alive in the regime's most oppressive moments.

These jokes kept them critical of the stupidity of the regime in which they lived, and the population's perception of the political and social changes that were happening around them, no matter how repressive the system was.

Until the moment when jokes were not enough and their individuals sought to act in favor of their freedom and their nations.

Modern Geopolitics: The "Inevitable" Nuclear Stupidity

Thucydides' Trap: An Impending U.S.-China Conflict?

Notwithstanding the problem of conflicts between Russia and the West, we have a global power at risk of being overtaken and seeing its hegemony fall, which could trigger disastrous consequences. The term "Thucydides' Trap", a recently popularized expression and taken from the following excerpt from the famous historical treatise *History of the Peloponnesian War* of Thucydides:

"It was the rise of Athens and the fear it instilled in Sparta that made war inevitable"

Thucydides, born in 460 BC, was an important Athenian historian and general, recognized for having written "History of the Peloponnesian War", where he describes with richness of detail and historical accuracy the war between Athens and Sparta, in the fifth century BC.

"To men who wish to see clearly what has occurred and will occur again, with all human possibility, in the same or similar manner."

During the war Thucydides was the general responsible for the protection of the region of Thrace and its main city, Amphipolis. In 424 B.C. the brilliant Spartan general Brasidas, in a swift and surprise attack, took the city of Amphipolis and consequently much of the region. Thucydides' defeat is not forgiven in Athens, and democracy decides to send him into exile. Brasidas is to this day recognized as a military genius and great orator, being compared by Plato to Achilles himself.

While his exile lasted, he became a historian. Thucydides, who recorded important events and speeches from the beginning of the war, was convinced that history should be a narrative of facts, given in rich detail and as close as possible to the real event, thus serving as a documented and reliable study of the past.

This was not yet common among the Greeks, Herodotus, his contemporary and famous historian, is recognized for the epic tones and exaggerations in his descriptions and for highlighting the actions of the Greek gods, taken in his narratives as real characters.

In the words of Thomas Hobbes, who made the first complete translation of his work from Greek into English, Thucydides was "the greatest historiographer who ever lived."

Considered the father of political realism and widely studied in the theories of international relations, he died shortly after the end of the war, leaving his work unfinished.

The Greek War

The Peloponnesian War began in 431 BC. The Peloponnesian League, led by Sparta, was the Greek coalition that resisted the Persian invasion in 479 BC, which made Sparta the leading city-state of all of Greece.

Athens, which had already begun to develop its powerful maritime empire, formed the Delian League, which under its leadership also fought the Persians, expanded territories and began to prosper and exert more and more influence in the region. As the Delian League grew and prospered, Sparta perceived with increasing dissatisfaction the threat Athens posed to its hegemony.

War, therefore, became inevitable. This war involved almost all the Greek states, an unprecedented number of resources, men, strategies and astonishing logistical investments.

An unparalleled development of naval power, its methods and strategies, with battles developing throughout Greece and Asia Minor.

Previously, battles did not require many combatants, without great strategies or distribution structures, and there were no diverse combat areas or strategies that were diverse and masterfully defined by both sides.

27 years after the start of the war, Athens succumbs to Sparta. The Athenian decline marks the definitive Spartan rise, but not without consequences for the entire Hellenic world. All these years of war, battles and conflicts caused incomparable wear and tear, the economic ruin of several Greek city-states and powers, military loss and total dismantling of Greek unity in the face of other empires.

While Greece was trying to recover, the Macedonian Empire, under the command of Philip II, Alexander's father, was organizing itself and becoming more and more powerful. Taking advantage of the post-war Greek instability and poverty, it invades and dominates almost all of Greece, thus ending the independence and freedom of most of the city-states of the Greek world.

Doomed to repeat the past?

With the onset of the Cold War, there was a great deal of interest from many researchers, historians, and military personnel about the wars of the past. These people noted the striking similarities between the conflicts of Athens and Sparta and the disputes of the United States and NATO vis-à-vis the Soviet Union and its allies.

In 1947, George C. Marshall, then the U.S. Secretary of State, says: "I seriously doubt that a man who has not at least recalled in his mind the time of the Peloponnesian War and the fall of Athens can reflect with full wisdom and deep conviction on certain issues of international relations today." This and other amazing comparisons can be seen in Donald Kagan's excellent article Thucydides: The Reinvention of History.

But the United States and the Soviet Union did not decline in conflict. They maintained constant disagreements and threats, a deep antipathy, but the Soviet Union had always been a military danger to the US and NATO, never a threat to their economic and financial power and influence. This would lead to the definitive fall of the Soviet Union in the early 1990s.

Despite all the recent chaos and the war in Ukraine caused by the conflicting interests between Russia and the West, and the war itself being an atrocious act of stupidity, we see the world still plunging into the global threat of a nuclear conflict between NATO and Russia, for dozens of reasons, whether "strategic", cultural or political, but threatening the fate of humanity as a whole. We can classify actions of the type of all Cipolla's laws of stupidity.

A different situation from what is happening today in U.S.-China relations. China offers the United States not only a military threat, but above all a threat to the previously uncontested economic and even political models of the entire West.

China's rise calls into question the functioning of Western democracy, its political structure, and what was held to be true in the development of countries' markets and economies.

It is the rise of a country with completely different models and structures from the current ones and that can surpass the current largest and most powerful economy in the world.

It is, in fact, a threat to a power never before seen in the modern world.

If the Thucydides Trap materializes when one power challenges the hegemony of another previously established power, we see the possibility of an inevitable war forming in the face of the fear that the military and economic rise of China (formerly Athens) offers to the military and economic hegemony of the United States (Sparta).

In "Destined For War: Can America and China Avoid Thucydides Trap?", Graham Allison argues that what defines or does not define the World Order for this generation is whether China and the United States can avoid falling into Thucydides' Trap.

Graham demonstrates that in the course of history, when, in these circumstances, other nations and countries have managed to avoid imminent armed conflict, enormous and painful adjustments have been required in the actions and decisions between rivals, both challenger and challenged.

Thucydides focused on showing the stress caused by the change in the balance of power and the tension generated by the steady growth of challenging power. And so there has never been such an upward and rapid change on the global stage as the evolution and growth of the Chinese.

Throughout history, most of the time when these patterns have been realized, rivalry between powers has resulted in wars and armed conflicts.

The greatest example may be the advent of World War I. England and France after the Industrial Revolution exercised their absolute hegemony and power, but the dizzying and unparalleled growth and development of the German Empire over the years caused such tension between the nations that the assassination of an Archduke was the trigger for the beginning of the largest and most violent war up to that time.

But Thucydides' Trap is not fatalistic, and the powers that be can avoid war if they act appropriately (avoiding stupidity).

During the great navigations, explorations and dangerous trade routes of the fifteenth century, the power struggles between Portugal and Spain were very intense.

In the early 1490s, the Spanish Empire was growing and increasing its maritime power and influence on trade routes around the world, threatening Portuguese autonomy and leadership and bringing the two nations to the brink of starting a war. Everything intensified further with the discovery of the New World, and conflict between the two nations for power and the new lands discovered seemed inevitable.

To prevent war there was even Papal intervention. With the leaders of the two nations sitting face to face and seeking solutions other than armed conflict, treaties and divisions of the newly discovered lands and partnerships emerged, such as the Bull Inter Caetera and the Treaty of Tordesillas.

The partnership between the two nations was maintained and lasted for a long time, making the strategic union and mutual protection between the two countries, the so-called Iberian Union, flourish. The treaties and agreements avoided conflict between the two powers.

Will we fall into a political-historical cycle of stupidity?

As much as China's influence increasingly extends across the Western Pacific, Xi Jinping has already demonstrated his plans for the new trade routes he intends to develop through other countries and continents and has attested to his increasingly expansive view of China's influence in the world.

The more China expands, the more it comes into conflict with the Americans and the countries already under their influence.

Not to mention the Chinese investment to have the largest naval armada in the world. The development of Chinese strategies and the quality and technology of warfare have improved significantly in recent years, with increasingly larger and more sophisticated ships and aircraft carriers, whose performance and capacity are as or as much greater than those of the West.

All this investment and growth demonstrates how much the Chinese plan to advance their influence around the world and keep Americans away from nearby territories, as if they decide to use force against Taiwan's autonomy.

While there is talk of a second Cold War, the interdependence of the American and Chinese economies elevates the conflicts to another level, which has most influenced the economy and global development in this century, the technological sector.

The battles fought in the cyber field demonstrate how fundamental the technology sector is to this modern Cold War, where the theft of data and information from governments and companies can be as harmful to a country as a nuclear detonation.

In the face of all this, the West fears that China could dominate technologies that are fundamental to development and the future, from blockchain and the internet, to AI and space travel. The world's economy and strategy are intimately linked to these clashes and innovations, with China increasingly dominating global technological and revolutionary development.

But it will all depend on China's continued growth. Government data has long been unreliable, and signs that its economy may be in trouble may show that the country's current model is not as effective as it has been in recent years.

If there is a slump in China's growth, the Communist Party leader may have two paths to take: calm the unbridled growth and try to put the house in order, or further increase the assertiveness of his plans and try to avoid at all costs the diminishing of the country's influence and power.

The rivalry between the U.S. and China will continue, the tendency of one to try to diminish and undermine the power and influence of the other. What remains to be seen is whether they will try to find non-stupid ways to balance their interests or will have an increasingly less friendly and more confrontational relationship, leading us, unfortunately, to the Thucydides Trap.

A Tale: Justice and Stupidity

Nothing as timeless as a work by William Shakespeare (1564-1616). In the story of The Merchant of Venice, written between 1596 and 1599 in the beautiful city of Venice in the fifteenth century, Bassanio asks Antonio for a loan of three thousand ducats so that he can court Porcia, a wealthy heiress. Antonio is wealthy, but all his money is in transportation to ventures outside of Venice.

So, to help his friend Bassanio, Antonio turns to the Jew Shylock to get the loan. Shylock was waiting for an opportunity to confront Antonio, since the latter had previously offended him, for being a Jew and for practicing usury (lending at interest), something that was considered a sin and forbidden among Christians, but allowed to Jews.

Shylock, in the contract, in trying to show good faith to Antonio, makes it the condition that he will not charge interest on the three thousand ducats, but if these are not paid in three months, Antonio must give a piece of his own flesh to the Jew. The ships with Antonio's fortune sink and he is unable to pay Shylock in time, causing the case to be taken to court to determine whether or not the condition will be enforced.

As soon as it is known about Antonio's misfortune, Shylock discovers that his daughter, Jessica, has run off with a friend of Antonio's taking part of his fortune, which makes Shylock furious.

Antonio's other friends try to convince Shylock not to collect the debt in contract, since Antonio has not been able to fulfill his part and, in a moment of anger, Shylock professes the famous speech "Hath not a jew eyes?", which we have an excerpt from below:

[...] "He disgraced me, and made me lose half a million, laughed at my losses, mocked my gains, mocked my nation, tore my bargains to pieces, chilled my friends, warmed my enemies. Why? Because I'm Jewish. Is it that a Jew has no eyes? Doesn't a Jew have hands, organs, dimensions, senses, affections, passions? Is he not fed with the same food, wounded with the same weapons, subject to the same diseases, healed by the same means, warmed and cooled by the same winter and summer, as a Christian? If they bite us, don't we bleed? If they tickle us, don't we laugh? If they poison us, don't we die? And if they do us wrong, shouldn't we take revenge?" [...]

The story is also told in the 2004 film, The Merchant of Venice, directed by Michael Radford, in which Shylock is masterfully played by Al Pacino.

Taken to court, Shylock demands that justice be done to him, and the contract be fulfilled. It proves to be irreducible and even indicates that Antonio's pound of flesh should be removed from the point closest to the heart. Porcia, now married to Bassanio, disguises herself as a man and introduces herself as Balthasar, a lawyer trying to find a resolution to the impasse.

It fails to offer double the amount that was owed; Shylock insists he just wants the contract to be fulfilled. Porcia, therefore, disguised as Balthasar, accepts the situation, but imposes that the removal of Antonio's flesh not be accompanied by any drop of blood. And, aligned with the doge, it asserts that the shedding of Christian blood would entail the confiscation of the Jew's fortune.

Interestingly, the way Jews have been depicted in English literature over the centuries, and this literature influencing other literatures and media, carries strong influence from Shakespeare and the interpretation of his Shylock.

With few variations, most of the country's pre-twentieth-century literary works show an excessively caricatured Jew, almost always depicted as a rich and avaricious individual, lascivious and only tolerated for the wealth and influence he possesses. This theme is extensively explored in the book The Fictive Jew in the Literature of England, by David Mirsky.

Shylock, cornered, revises his position and claims to accept the money offered, but the judge denies him, because he has already refused this agreement. Now, for having conspired against the life of a Venetian, it is decided that Shylock will have to hand over half of his goods to Antonio and the other half to the State.

Anthony, finally, denies his part, stating as a condition Shylock's conversion to Christianity, thus forcing him, in addition to practically losing all his possessions, also to renounce his faith.

In 2016, the famous U.S. Supreme Court Justice Ruth Bader Ginsburg and other fellow justices staged a reenactment of Shylock's trial in Venice, giving a different ending to Shakespeare's plot.

If the situation were the other way around, and Shylock was the one who had to and put his own skin at risk, would the judges of the time even hesitate to fulfill the contract to the letter and, consequently, take the meat from the Jew? With this questioning we can bring the famous phrase attributed to Niccolò Machiavelli (1469-1527): "To friends everything, to enemies the law".

We come to perceive a justice that always tends to the side of the most favored, the most powerful and influential, the "dominant."

In this sense, the laws should provide that everyone is equal, and the judgments, the fulfillment of contracts, are fair. But who will watch over the one who makes the laws? (Quis custodiet ipsos custodes?) Whoever makes these laws, whoever interprets them, will not do so that some will be more favored than others when it is convenient? What guarantees that this will not be the case?

We see these problems in all the Republics. More closely, in ours. Either in the ordinary court or, recurrently through the media, in the Supreme Court.

Our country, particularly, with an immense Constitution, full of buts, amendments and variations, leaving a judicial system that is already slow, even more complex and open to points of view, creating more loopholes for interpretations, each interpretation for a moment, or who, when it is convenient. The Latin maxim of the Roman senator Tacitus (56 A.D. – 120 A.D.) fits us well: "Corruptissima republica plurimae leges" (The more corrupt the state, the more laws it has).

These subjects are extensively studied in Contract Theory

Being an area of Economics, specifically microeconomics, Contract Theory aims to understand how contractual arrangements and their interactions are constituted by economic actors, whether they are just individuals, companies or nations.

It is also studied how unpredictability affects these agreements, bringing to the study of this theory, in addition to concepts of economic analysis of law and micro and macroeconomics itself, also probability and the understanding of algorithms and models to better understand decision-making and try to calculate its effects and consequences.

Well-defined contracts, regardless of what the negotiation or its objective is, are capable of optimizing the relationship and the returns of those involved, making these relationships more fruitful, influencing all the processes of a system that provides improvement to an entire sector, a business model or even the functioning of the entire economy.

By minimizing uncertainties, influenced by information asymmetry, and making the best potential execution of agreements and contracts, we start to develop a business environment with much more fluidity, performance and efficiency.

There are many less abstract and more applicable concepts in Contract Theory. The famous Neumann-Morgenstern Utility Theorem is used in his studies, for example, which is the basis for the Expected Utility Theory.

Consequently, Contract Theory is profusely analyzed and applied in another very important area for Economics, and just as interesting, Game Theory. The Nash equilibrium is a good model for this applicability, and all studies on Decision Theory.

It seeks to find solutions to the classic and common Adverse Selection Problem, a problem that occurs when one of the parties involved in a transaction knows things relevant to that transaction, but which are unknown to the other interested party.

There are more axiomatic concepts and principles, such as the term "Pacta Sunt Servanda" (pacts must be observed) – implying that a contract is actually binding between the parties. The contract binds the parties within the limits that the law imposes, of course. By this principle, Shylock today could not enforce a contract that would threaten Antonio's life, no matter how much signed contracts must be strictly fulfilled.

Or the principle of "Rebus Sic Stantibus" – implying that contracts stand 'if the present situation remains the same'. Unforeseeable and surprising situations, which prove to be really difficult to calculate, and affect one of the parties (a natural disaster, for example), can cause the contract to be revised or even cease to be valid. The shipwreck of Antonio's fortune, for example, could be a model of the applicability of this principle, causing the contract to be revised. These analyses and this concept are the basis for the so-called Theory of Unpredictability.

Economists Oliver Hart of Harvard University and Bengt Holmström of the Massachusetts Institute of Technology (MIT) were awarded the 2016 Nobel Prize in Economic Sciences for their contributions to contract theory.

Kenneth Arrow is also an important economist (and winner of the 1972 Nobel Prize in Economic Sciences) whose studies helped in the evolution of this theory.

Therefore, in order to deal with the timeless injustice of the world, one in which the weakest and most distant from power never seem to be treated as equals, however ignoble and stupid they may be, and in which Justice demonstrates that it has its own preferences, we need to better understand how the relationships and interactions between individuals and organizations can achieve maximum efficiency. making them really fair, balanced and bringing what is due, not only at the mercy of stupidity and other people's interests. The world needs to remember that equality, justice and freedom are more than words, they are perspectives, and that they must be watched. But, unfortunately, for this world, George Orwell's classic phrase still seems to prevail:

"All animals are equal, but some animals are more equal than others" – George Orwell in Animal Farm, 1945.

Noticing Stupidity: The Power of the Word

Rub (Busillis)

It is a masculine noun, consisting of the most important point of a question; the essence of a problem; Difficulty: We still can't find the rub. (From Latin, busillis).

When one knows one's own language well, an interest in the deeper origin and meaning of words arises. Thus, etymology becomes an increasingly interesting study, making us improve our speech, comprehension of words, and oratory.

During the dark Middle Ages, the people who had the greatest access to knowledge, information, books, and the Latin language itself were the friars.

The friars were in charge of translating ancient books, mostly in Latin and Greek, into modern European languages, to facilitate studies, develop analyses, or simply have the book or material translated into their native language.

However, no matter how well you know the language, it is not always easy to translate something, in the midst of different forms of writing, own terms, locations, historical moments or simply come across completely new words, even more so when you are a Portuguese medieval friar.

It can be found in human culture several references about the quick resolution of problems, almost as a trigger. The need to recognize patterns and thus resolve any complication quickly is, in fact, a trait that has always impelled humanity.

Perhaps, one of the oldest and most famous reference stories that addresses the topic is one in which the protagonist is none other than Alexander the Great.

It is said that Gordius, an ancient king of Phrygia (a region that is now in Turkey), tied a rope with a knot on a large column in a temple dedicated to Zeus that would have been impossible to untie. Some time later, when the Oracle was consulted on the subject, it was prophesied that whoever untied such a knot would rule the world.

More than five hundred years later, without anyone being able to untie the knot, Alexander the Great, passing through the region and hearing the story, became curious, and went to the temple of Zeus to see such a feat. After some time analyzing the spine and the rope, he unsheathed his sword and cut the knot.

Whether it was just a legend or not, years later Alexander established himself as the owner of one of the greatest empires in all of history. The term "cutting the Gordian knot" has become synonymous with solving a complex problem simply, effectively, right at its root.

Another famous secular occurrence about a feat of the same kind is the story of Columbus' Egg.

The French, on the other hand, have a famous term for recognizing a pattern and, consequently, quickly finding the central focus of a problem: "Cherchez la Femme" (yes, a bit sexist).

The expression comes from the 1854 book Les Mohicans de Paris, by Alexandre Dumas, father. The original passage reads:

"Il y a une femme dans toute les affaires; aussitôt qu'on me fait un rapport, je dis: 'Cherchez la femme'."

"There is always a woman involved in every case. As soon as they bring me a report, I immediately say, 'Look for the woman.'"

The phrase sums up a commonplace of detective stories: no matter what the problem is, the motive will almost always be wrapped around a woman.

The term 'Cherchez la femme' has become common in the French language, always as a synonym for 'look for the root of the problem'.

To return to the friars: we Portuguese speakers also have a term of our own that implies 'the root of the problem'.

'Busilis' is a word whose existence is due to the mistranslation of some friar Portuguese sometime during the Middle Ages.

The term 'busilis' is believed to have originated from the Latin misinterpretation of the term "In diebus illis", which, from a literal meaning, represents "in those days" or "at that time".

The friars in question found the term "in diebus illis magnis plenae", that is, "in those days there was an abundance of great things", however, the space between the words was not well defined and the term ended up being interpreted as:

"Indie 'Busillis' Magnis Plenae".

"Indie" would be one of the Latin terms for India, and the mistranslation would look something like this:

"India "busillis" abundance of great things", leaving the word 'busillis', which did not exist until then, untranslated.

The meaning of such a word became a nuisance to the friars, who ended up associating the term with the concept of 'root of a problem' or 'point of great difficulty'.

Even more so, after some time, when the friars realized the mistake they had made.

To recognize the moment of the birth of a word, a totally new term, is to recognize the importance and characteristics of our language, it is to understand, in fact, its importance and its beauty, which every language, no matter its origin, possesses.

Parsimony

It is a feminine noun, it represents the act of saving, of saving, of spending moderately; economy, sobriety. Quality of which is meager. (From Latin, parsimoniae).

Often, in a relentless search for patterns and answers, we create rules, using our own experience and cognition, to try to avoid mistakes, predict them, or calculate the consequences of our actions or situations.

It's human nature to fear the future and the consequences of our actions and decisions, so it's natural to do our best to try to lessen our vulnerability to unpredictability.

Imagine, therefore, a pattern, which fits practically every possible line of reasoning, which facilitates the resolution of a problem or decision-making, always seeking to ensure final success.

One of these is the Law of Parsimony (Lex Parsimoniae). This law, also known as Occam's Razor, was devised by William of Occam, an English Franciscan friar who lived between the eleventh and twelfth centuries. William was a staunch defender of individual freedom and free will, believing that each individual would have the need to make their own choices, without the intervention of state or religion to define the aspects of their life and their own decisions. He believed that the simplicity of freedom was the answer to harmony and the right way of things.

The Law of Parsimony is based on the premise that the universe, nature itself, is economic. Nature never makes an effort beyond what is necessary, its goals and ends are always by the quickest, simplest, most direct means. There is no overexertion or loss of energy. As da Vinci said, "simplicity is the last degree of sophistication."

The applicability of this concept is extremely wide-ranging, Parsimony influences from the scientific method, the basis of all scientific research and theories in the world, to concepts and ideologies of Modern Economics.

Differential and Integral Calculus, like several other discoveries, have undergone numerous reformulations in the course of new research and improvements until reaching our current limit of understanding on the subject. And our understanding has always, throughout each century of studies and new discoveries, become more and more parsimonious and simple to understand and/or apply. Simplicity is a consequence of experience, creativity and the ability to synthesize and better organize the knowledge one has on a given subject.

Reinforcing da Vinci, Saint-Exupéry states that "perfection is not achieved when there is nothing left to add, but when there is nothing more that can be taken away".

Elegant, laconic and even childish, Occam's Razor inspires beauty and aspires to the perfection of things. His concept was already discussed and was thought of by several others long before Occam himself. From Aristotle to Maimonides, from philosophers to scientists, there is a wide range of thinkers who saw the action of nature through simplicity and that when there are two paths to a conclusion, the simplest, thrifty, is the closest to the correct. Always beware of logical errors and fallacies, obviously.

Now, understanding the terms busily (the essence of a problem) and parsimony (the simplest path to a resolution), we can ask ourselves: is there a simple and efficient solution to solve essentially all problems? (Perhaps, specifically, from the Economy?)

We are trying to use another term, not yet mentioned: **panacea**.

Panacea

This time from the Greek, *panakeia*, in ancient Greek religion, was the goddess of universal medicine, daughter of Asclepius, Greek god of medicine.

It was said that the goddess possessed a potion with which to heal the sick. This brought about the concept of a "panacea" in medicine, a substance with the alleged property of curing all diseases. The term also came to be used figuratively to mean "something used to solve all problems."

At this point we know the exact term to refer to what we are looking for, but does it exist?

In Physics, one of the questions that keeps researchers up at night is a possible way to integrate Classical Mechanics, General Relativity and Quantum Mechanics. Particles and bodies have unique particularities when observed by different theories and fields of study. The physics of planets and the physics of the motions of subatomic particles are different and obey different mathematical rules and concepts, which do not reconcile with each other. A single theory that would explain the two Mechanics and integrate it with the same set of laws is the panacea of this science. It would explain everything from quantum movements to the emergence and structures of the universe, helping to explain and develop several other researches, hypotheses, technologies and would impact humanity as a whole.

The closest thing to a "Theory of Everything" in physics is about M-Theory (String Theory is within it), but we are a little far from finding an answer to that riddle.

For, perhaps, not everything can really be explained. Gödel's famous Incompleteness Theorems state that when it comes to a union of mathematical concepts too deep to try to explain some theory or excessively robust and complex structures, mathematics itself will find inherent limitations in its bases to interpret and explain the phenomenon completely or satisfactorily.

If there is no panacea for problems in mathematics or physics, there probably is no panacea in the simplest and most social human interactions.

Understanding how much words can contain meanings and senses, we should understand what is demonstrably stupid to use it, and if it is not just expressing absurd ideas or ideals, telling a lie or demonstrating a logic completely on some topic, the stupidest way to use words would be **fallacies**.

Fallacy

Before going to the fallacy, perhaps Rhetoric and Dialectics are one of the most treated subjects in all philosophy. Possibly in the same proportion as they are fallaciously quoted and discussed.

A Bit of Dialectics
Dialectics has several interpretations, almost one for each philosopher. For Plato, dialectics is one of the main paths to truth. The discussion where one questions and through argumentation one comes to the conclusion of where we would see the truth.

Aristotle, on the other hand, saw dialectics as the elevation of dialogue, when the discussions were superior and in search of a greater truth, but which, unfortunately, could never be proven.

Immanuel Kant interprets dialectics as a delusion. Kant advocated questioning the real and rational in the immediate way it is interpreted.

The Hegelian Dialectic is perhaps the most studied at the present time. Georg Hegel devoted a good part of his works to dealing with dialectics, even having his own terms for it. Hegel interprets dialectics in three fundamental points:

i) **Thesis:** corresponds to the subject dealt with and questioned.
ii) **Antithesis:** corresponds to the detailed definition or negation of the Thesis.
iii) **Synthesis:** corresponds to a result, a new interpretation of the facts presented, a new vision of the truth that was not seen until then.

A Bit of Rhetoric
Rhetoric, unlike dialectics, is reserved for the art (some see it as a science) of arguing, discussing, and persuading. Aristotle even said that Rhetoric and Dialectic were opposites.

The fine line between Rhetoric and Oratory, one born of the other, would be the focus of (Greek) rhetoric being on argumentation and that of (Roman) oratory being eloquence. The Rhetoric is divided into:

i) Ethos: the techniques and concepts that the speaker uses to convince and influence the audience about his or her qualification and mastery of the subject. Social aspects, posture and many other conscious and subconscious factors influence the listener.

ii) Pathos: the use of characteristics that denote emotion, fervor, or even passion to influence the listener's judgment.

Following several techniques to arouse these feelings in the audience, maintain attention and cause enthusiasm.

iii) Logos: the applicability and use of reason, true or not, to build credibility and demonstrate truthfulness to discourse. Demonstrate mastery of the theme, with the construction of an information network bringing characteristics and data, causing acceptance and credibility to the arguments.

Complementing with Logic
These two liberal arts would be nothing if it weren't for a third and equally important liberal art: Logic.

Without Logic, the arguments, questions, and conclusions, both of the philosophical and metaphysical digressions of Dialectics and of the political studies and civil treatises of Rhetoric, would be meaningless.

If it weren't for logic, all these treaties would have no meaning. Their argument would be a mistake, a false line of reasoning that would be nothing more than the simplest demagoguery to convince an audience or win a speech. And not seeking the truth and questioning the facts as is the oldest sense of these arts.

To the fact of a 'false line of reasoning' with a vile or dishonest aim, the ancients also had a term for it: Fallacy.

Fallacy is false logic, insistent argumentation that convinces, that seems true, but uses incorrect and inconsistent logic.

These arguments are more frequent and closer than one might think. We ourselves, when we try to convince someone of our point of view, no doubt we have used or will still use fallacious arguments.

Whether it's the doubts of the great philosophers, the exchange of ideas between people or even the resolution of a problem, escaping from fallacious logic is, without a doubt, a path that will take you closer to the truth.

Let's look at some examples of fallacies

I) Argumentum ad ignorantiam
Trying to prove something out of ignorance as to its validity. Just because you don't know if something is true doesn't mean it's false, and vice versa.

E.g.: No one has been able to prove that God does not exist, therefore he exists.

II) Argumentum ad antiquitatem
Claiming that something is true or good only because it is old or because it has "always been that way."

Ex: Our grandparents educated this way, so it's the right way to educate.

III) Argumentum ad novitatem
Arguing that the new is always better, without actual logic.

E.g.: In philosophy, Socrates is already outdated. It's better Sartre, because he's more recent.

IV) Argumentum ad misericordiam
Also called an appeal to godliness. It consists in the recourse to pity or related feelings, such as sympathy and compassion, so that the conclusion is accepted, even though the pity is not related to the subject or the conclusion of the argument.

From the argument ad misericordiam derives the argumentum ad infantium – "Do this for the children." Emotion is used to persuade people to support (or intimidate them into rejecting) an argument based on emotion rather than evidence or reasons.

V) Argumentum ad nauseam

It is the application of constant repetition and the incorrect belief that the more you say something, the more correct it is.

E.g.: If William insists so much that his teacher is bad, then she is.

VI) Argumentum ad hominem

Instead of the arguer proving the falsity of the statement, he attacks the person who made the statement.

E.g.: If it was Luiz who said that, it's certainly false.

It uses the fact that Luiz said something to emphasize that it is false just because it is Luiz.

VII) Argumentum ad lapidem

Dismissing a statement as absurd but without proof.

E.g.: João, a former president, is accused of corruption and defends himself by saying: "This accusation is a lie from the Federal Revenue Service!".

Based on what? Where is the evidence to the contrary?

VIII) Tu quoque

It consists of admitting a mistake that others also make, as if it were an excuse.

E.g.: You have also been charged with corruption.

IX) Ignoratio elenchi
It consists of using arguments that may be valid to reach a conclusion that has no relation to the arguments used. An attempt is being made to prove something other than what we are talking about.

E.g.:

It is through taxes that the government obtains money to help the most needy citizens;
Data shows that there are still many people in need;
So the solution is for the government to raise taxes.
This argument does not prove what it wants, which is that the needs of the citizens should be solved by raising taxes.

X) Plurium interrogationum
It occurs when a simple answer to a complex question is required.

E.g.: What are we going to do with this criminal? Kill or imprison?

It's a false dilemma.

XI) Scotsman's Fallacy
Making a claim about a characteristic of a group and, when confronted with a contrary example, asserting that that example does not really belong to the group.

E.g.:

No Scotsman puts sugar in his porridge.

Well, I have a Scottish friend who does that.
Oh yes, but no "real" Scotsman puts it on.
The fallacy does not occur if there is a justification for the argument.

XII) Conspiracy Theory
E.g.: An ancient, secret group controls all aspects of life on Earth. There is no proof of the existence of this group. And this only happens because an ancient, secret group controls every aspect of life on Earth.

XIII) Appeal to the consequence
To consider a premise to be true or false according to its consequence is desired.

E.g.: You must be good to others or you will go to Hell.

The premise is taken for granted only because the conclusion pleases or frightens us.

XIV) Appeal to ridicule
Ridiculing an argument as a way to overturn it.

E.g.: If the theory of evolution were true, it would mean that your great-great-grandfather would be a gorilla.

XV) Appeal to authority
An argument based on an appeal to some recognized authority to prove the premise. It's the famous "do you know who you're talking to?".

E.g., If Aristotle said that the Sun revolves around the Earth in one of the celestial spheres, then it is certainly true.

These were just a few examples of a countless number of fallacies. Knowing the basis of the logic of argumentation and, of course, common sense allied to all this, are the principles for not falling into empty and biased speeches, which are even so common in our old politics.

Some stupid (and some not so stupid) examples of the use of words

"I believe he is peace in our time"
- Neville Chamberlain (British Prime Minister, in 1939) on Adolf Hitler

Chamberlain said the fateful phrase after signing the Munich Agreement, an agreement that virtually ignored Nazi Germany's recent invasions of Eastern Europe, the annexation of Austria and followed the 'Policy of Appeasement', a policy that consented to the path of submitting to Nazi impositions in the belief that this could avoid war.

Less than a year after the Munich Agreement, Germany invaded Poland, demonstrating the failure of the policy of submission, forcing Britain to declare war on the Third Reich. A few months later, Chamberlain is replaced by Winston Churchill as Prime Minister.

On Chamberlain and his stance towards the Nazis, Churchill wisely stated:

"Between dishonor and war, thou hast chosen dishonor, and thou shalt have war"

We often overlook the power that words possess. In our routines, in work meetings, on a date, over coffee. We do not know what it can do to those who listen to us, how much it can sadden, rejoice, inflame nationalist wills or call citizens to war and the defense of freedom.

If in our daily lives the way words are used is immensely important, it is unquestionable how much more powerful words and their influence on nations, international relations and political discourses can be and have even greater consequences.

We can see this from the speeches of politicians around the world, and the consequences that their often inappropriate words bring. Whether it's from Donald Trump influencing global markets with his tweets or the interviews and comments of politicians closest to him on social media and their consequences for the country. Comments that often cause national or international crises or economic instability, which could be completely avoided with a little more common sense and the better employability of words.

In his masterful and perhaps most difficult "We Shall Fight on the Beaches" speech, delivered in June 1940, a few weeks after the Fall of France to the Nazis, Churchill had the very difficult duty of describing the French military disaster and warning the British people of the imminent invasion attempt by Nazi Germany, all without raising any doubts about the future victory of the Allies.

"We will go all the way. We will fight in France. We will fight on the seas and oceans, we will fight with growing confidence and growing strength in the air, we will defend our island, whatever the cost. We will fight on the beaches, we will fight on the landing grounds, we will fight in the fields and in the streets, we will fight on the hills; we will never surrender (...)"

- Excerpt from Winston Churchill's "We Shall Fight on the Beaches"

On the frontlines of World War II, in addition to the thousands of soldiers who perished against tyranny and defending the freedom of their nations, were Churchill's intelligent and necessary speeches. Whether it was to proclaim civilian ships, to pick up almost 400,000 British and French soldiers trapped by the Nazis on the beaches of Dunkirk, or to "write" the Atlantic Charter and make an alliance with the US against the Axis Powers, or to make a speech of hope and strength for the British and the world after Continental Europe fell to the Nazis.

In "The Verve and the Poison of Winston Churchill" by Dominique Enright, we can find a compilation of phrases, excerpts from Churchill's speeches or comments, from his most in-depth analyses of politics to more ironic and funny tirades about his fellow parliamentarians or situations he went through during his life and in the positions he held.

Once asked about the requirements a politician should fulfill, Churchill promptly replied:

"The ability to predict what's going to happen tomorrow, next week and next year. And the ability to explain later why none of that happened."
At a press conference in Cairo in 1943, he admitted:

"I always avoid prophesying in advance because the best policy is to predict after the event has already taken place."

Many times in history words have been the most powerful forces in the face of the most powerful enemies, and they have brought hope and fervor to diverse peoples against the tyranny of their executioners.

Laconia is a region south of the Peloponnese and its capital is the historic city of Sparta. The Spartans, among other peoples, were known for the region where they lived, so they were also laconic. The term laconic, in the course of time, became an adjective of a succinct, brief person, of few words.

This characteristic became a hallmark of this people, and the term has lasted for more than 2,000 years. However, a little discretion is not enough to create a term and mark history. There are several accounts of Spartan laconism, both in battle and in not-so-hostile situations.

Leonidas, the Spartan king during the Battle of Thermopylae, like a good Spartan, was laconic and quick in his answers, usually simple but very well applied.

Xerxes, the Persian Emperor, sent an emissary to negotiate with Leonidas. Asking only for '*Land and Water*'; if the Spartan king accepted the term and yielded it to him, it meant, basically, an agreement of total submission to the Achaemenid Empire.

When Leonidas refused to submit, the messenger told him, *"Our arrows will be so numerous that they will block the sunlight."* Leonidas quickly replies:

"So much the better, we'll fight in the shadows!"

An Athenian woman once asked Gorgo, wife of Leonidas and queen of Sparta, why the Spartans were the only Greeks who ruled their men; To which she promptly replied:

"Why, because we're the only ones who give birth to real men."

It was common when the sons of Sparta took leave of their mothers to go to war, they would say to them, "My son, come back with your shield, or on top of it," that is, come back victorious or dead.

However, there are stories that mark more than others.

Philip II, the Great King of the Macedonian Empire, was forming what would become, in the hands of his son Alexander the Great, one of the largest and most powerful armies of all time.

The Macedonian king always aimed to dominate Greece, and taking advantage of the weakening of the city-states by internal wars in the Peloponnese, he attacked. Before long, the Macedonian king ruled over almost all of Greece's city-states, including Athens. Sparta was then the last free Greek power.

Philip II, before planning any attack on the Spartan power, sent them an emissary with a letter that, in addition to demonstrating his power and squandering the recent conquests of his Empire, including his greatest historical rival, Athens, said something like:

"I advise you Spartans to subdue your city without further delay, because IF we invade your city, we will burn your farms, destroy your temples, massacre your people, and ultimately destroy it."

The Spartan Senate sent a letter replying to Philip II with the following *simple* writing:

"IF"

"If" they invade, "if" they manage to get past the Spartan soldiers, "if" they manage to cross the city gates. This simple "if" sent by the Spartan senate meant and frightened more than any erudite speech by any politician in Athens.

The repercussions of this message to the mighty Macedonian Empire were so great throughout Greece that Philip II never attempted to invade Sparta. He advanced his armies to the Persians, but never south of the Peloponnese.

Only the one who could completely dominate the entire region of Greece and impose his hegemony would be his successor, Alexander, many years after the event.

From Churchill's speeches to Spartan laconism, his discipline and acumen with words make it more than evident that power, influence and the ability to communicate, confidence and clarity in conveying a message or defending a point of view are undeniable characteristics of a good leader. Words have the power to start wars, to prevent them, to bring chaos, or prosperity. Influencing decisions, developing situations and solving problems is far beyond theoretical or methodological knowledge, stupidity itself, but it can be, yes, essentially, in the way we deal with words. As Churchill concludes:

"Of all the talents bestowed upon men, none is so precious as the grace of oratory. Whoever enjoys it possesses a power more enduring than that of a great king."

Is there, then, a Hope against Stupidity? Education!

In 2004 there was one of the greatest natural catastrophes in modern history: The Indian Ocean Tsunami, caused by a 9.3 earthquake, where there were about 230 thousand deaths in the 14 affected countries, displaced approximately 1.5 million people and caused billions of dollars in damage and losses to the affected nations.

In this same area where this tsunami had occurred, similar occurrences were repeated in 1797, 1833, 1843 and 1861. In 1833, the Krakatoa tsunami killed nearly 40,000 people.

An earthquake and tsunami in Chile in 1960 killed 6,000 people. A set of long-range sensors was installed in the Pacific Ocean to predict and warn coastal populations of such earthquakes and threats, but nothing like this was built in the Indian Ocean. The governments of the region, of course, opposed the proposal.

Indonesia, the country hardest hit by the tsunami because of its proximity to the quake's epicenter, could do little to try to minimize the catastrophe.

However, other distant countries, such as Sri Lanka where there were 35,000 deaths, India with approximately 15,000, 8,000 in Thailand and more 1,000 in more distant places, could have saved these approximately 60,000 people if they had a system for warning and analyzing the tectonic plates in the Indian Ocean.

From the start of the earthquake, the waves took up to two hours to reach the tourist islands of Phuket in Thailand, and even longer to reach Sri Lanka. It wouldn't take more than 10 minutes to empty a beach.

The Japanese, the hardest hit by tsunamis of any other Pacific people, have a three-minute warning system and consider themselves capable of evacuating coastal areas in ten minutes. Still, there were 239 dead when the huge wave hit Hokkaido in 1993. But this relatively small number can demonstrate how effective these warning systems can be.

Years before the tragedy, a Thai meteorologist claimed that the resort complex in Phuket could be exceptionally vulnerable should another tsunami hit the coast.

He suggested installing sensors and alarms in hotels and also recommended building further away from the beach. (The costs for installing the sensors would be no more than $30 million, a very small cost compared to the billions in damage caused by the catastrophe and the lives that could have been saved.)

For raising such a problem, the meteorologist was transferred to another department on the government's pretext that the mere mention of tsunamis could drive away tourists. These details are very well described in the book Tsunami: The World's Most Terrifying Natural Disaster, by Geoff Tibballs.

Tilly Smith, a 10-year-old British woman at the time, had a better attitude.
Tilly was on holiday with her family in Ami Khao Beach, north of Phuket, Thailand, when she noticed strange signs in the sea.

"I didn't know what a tsunami was, but seeing your daughter so scared makes her think something serious must be going on."

Penny Smith – Tilly's mother to The Sun

A few weeks earlier, at school in Oxshott, England, his geography teacher had shown him videos of a 1980 tsunami, explained the phenomenon, the causes, and how to recognize one. The mother describes what happened next:

"Tilly said she had studied it at school. She talked about plate tectonics and undersea earthquakes as she became more and more hysterical. At the end she was screaming for us all to get off the beach."

Tilly, only 10 years old, saved more than 100 people; His morning on that beach was to try to convince as many tourists as possible to flee as quickly as possible, while the negligence and negligence of governments spared no one. More than 60,000 people could have been saved if these governments had been more prudent and diligent.

This is just one more example of the need to police the priorities of governments, their management and, above all, to demonstrate the importance of education and knowledge in the face of the power that individuals have to make a difference, better than entire governments.

Epilogue
Dealing with a Black Swan or Don't limit yourself just because you're stupid

We believe that, many times, if we are guided by logic, mathematics, probability or any other reasoning tools, we will be able to predict or "calculate" situations, events, catastrophes or spectacular shifts in the market, in the economy, in politics or even in personal life; however, we have already learned from the Laws of Stupidity that we will invariably be exposed to individuals or our own stupid decisions.

But, many times, we don't take into account how unreal these paths can be, guided by our view of the world, our subjectivity, by the non-understanding or non-perception of all the variables that really exist, or simply accepting that there is no way to predict the future and realize how much any way of trying to do it, using scientific models or not, It's closer to induction than anything else.

In The Black Swan, published in 2007, Nassim Taleb denotes the belief of Europeans, until 1697, that there were only white swans when, in that year, a black swan was sighted, for the first time, in Australia.

Taleb defines a Black Swan as a rare event that has a major impact on society and is somehow explainable, but beyond that, it would be virtually impossible to predict just by looking at the past. It was impossible to predict the existence of black swans until one was first seen.

Rare events, such as the first black swan, or so many others in the course of history (from wars, inventions, financial crises, political crises or even pandemics) occur more often than we imagine and, naturally, our minds are not programmed to deal with what is out of the routine or the status quo, so we try to explain the situation in the most comforting way possible. Since it is not at all pleasant for the human mind to deal with unplanned or unforeseen events.

There are patterns for recognizing such events. The first and foremost characteristic is its complete or partial unpredictability. When it occurs, it causes a huge impact and, after it happens, the most varied explanations emerge trying to affirm it as less random and more predictable than it really was.

According to Taleb, we do not have prior perception of such phenomena because human beings are programmed to learn specific things, to stick to them, and not to think in generalities and varied scenarios. Thus, we cannot clearly assess the opportunities, nor are we open enough to believe those who can calculate seemingly improbable scenarios.

The Logical Flaw of the Stupid: The Problem of Induction

The problem of induction is the cognitive-philosophical question concerning inductive reasoning, which can often be a generalization about a topic or a non-deductive prediction (i.e., a prediction based on non-rational or logical impressions) and which could lead to truth or knowledge itself.

In view of this, the problem of induction can be defined in two flaws:

i) Generalize: To assume that what has been previously analyzed only empirically becomes the default truth and therefore there is no possibility of changing or varying in the future, or that everything is always that way (e.g., returning to the logic that "all the swans we have seen are white, and therefore all the swans that exist are white", before the discovery of the black swan);

ii) Presupposition: Starting from the premise that future events will always occur as they were in the past and that situations will remain the same, practically in inertia (for example, that the laws of physics will manifest themselves as they have always been observed, but that today their structures have been questioned by Quantum Mechanics).

The Scientific Method itself is based on inductive logic and classical empiricism, but we should, at the very least, accept that there is a considerable chance that current analyses and interpretations may change over time. In short, there is no absolute truth, much less an infinitely constant environment in which there will be no variations or instabilities.

Although the Problem of Induction has been studied since the skeptical philosophers of Ancient Greece, it is David Hume who brings it up with a more scientific analysis. Hume states that one of the bases of the problem is to conclude which are the best inductive methods, when we note that it is not possible to find any objective difference between good and bad inductive methods.

Thus, induction is an inference and can only lead to a conclusion that has a limited degree of probability of being correct.

In his Treatise on Human Nature, Hume asserts that the relation that probabilistic connections have to what actually occurs depends on habits of the observer's mind, but not necessarily on his or her experience of the world. A philosophical solution to these points is very well addressed in Karl Popper's concept of Falsifiability.

Black Swans are events that cause major transformations on several levels, whether it is the destruction of a sector in the financial market or a political crisis. The effects of these events can profoundly affect some people, however others can go through virtually unscathed.

There is only one way to protect yourself from the impacts of such an event: information. The more informed you are, generally speaking, the less chance you have of being surprised by a Black Swan. The more ignorant and scattered you are, the more likely you are to be surprised and affected by these theoretically unpredictable situations.

A Black Swan can transform the entire understanding of centuries-old concepts and change the course of humanity forever. When Copernicus proposed that the Earth is not the center of the universe, there were consequences, not only for religion at the time, but for society and science.

Just like the Peloponnesian War, the Black Death or the Industrial Revolution. All of these events shaped the world in their own way and paved the way for a cultural shift in society as a whole. Swans like these change previously seemingly unshakable concepts and accelerate changes in the world about all their consequences.

Accepting the Improbable as a Reality

It is essential to be open to the possibility of unplanned or really surprising results in the journeys we take. It takes the addiction out of our minds of having no expectation for change and definitely takes us out of our comfort zone and keeps us on our toes.

The surprising should always be seen as a real possibility. This will make it easier for us to notice a Black Swan when we come across one. It would be like looking for a new way to the Indies (something you expected) and finding something you definitely didn't expect (discovering another continent).

There is a law in statistics, called the law of iterated expectations. It asserts that the expectation of attaining knowledge by itself is equivalent to knowledge itself.

This law acts as follows in the human mind: When I expect something to happen in a certain time, I already have as a premise, in the present, that it will happen.

If you believe today that you will make certain choices in the future, or that you will take certain directions in your life, you have practically already made them. It's a logic we shouldn't get stuck with. This is also analyzed in the logical-philosophical concept of Self-Fulfilling Prophecy.

To deal with a Black Swan or even benefit from one of them, in addition to staying informed about the changes in the world and its open mindset to all the possibilities that life exposes us to, we must be as little vulnerable as possible to situations that can affect us excessively. What you believe could affect your life irreversibly should be well analyzed and properly evidenced.

When it comes to the uncertain, we should always be skeptical of other people's predictions and be open-minded to any events. Never discredit something just because it seems unlikely, whether it's good, uh, or just plain stupid.

Expose yourself to situations where positive events can happen and they will happen; Be aware of the world's transitions and its tendencies and you will be able to perceive the next failures and changes that will arise. And as Taleb states, we shouldn't try to make so many predictions, we'd just be spending our time and energy on something we haven't really mastered. That would be stupid.

Part 2 - Neurosis

Prologue
Neurosis... What does it consist of?

We are all neurotic. To a greater or lesser extent, with a greater or lesser harmful impact on ourselves and others.

The human mind is a vast and mysterious field, filled with riddles that defy our comprehension and at the same time instigate our curiosity. Psychoanalysis, from its inception, has set out to decipher these enigmas, delving into the depths of the unconscious to unravel the secrets that reside there. Among the many phenomena that psychoanalysis has set out to study, neurosis occupies a prominent place, being an intriguing manifestation of the emotional and psychological complexities of the human being.

Sigmund Freud, the father of psychoanalysis, devoted much of his career to studying and understanding neuroses. In his seminal work Studies on Hysteria (1895), co-authored with Josef Breuer, Freud presented some of the earliest and most influential case studies that would come to shape his understanding of neuroses. These cases not only illuminated the mechanisms underlying neurotic symptoms, but also laid the foundation for the theory and practice of psychoanalysis.

Neurosis, as Freud defined it, refers to a wide range of psychological disorders that manifest themselves through physical and emotional symptoms. These symptoms are often the result of unconscious conflicts and repressed desires that express themselves in symbolic and often disconcerting ways. The most common forms of neurosis include hysteria, obsessive-compulsive neurosis, phobia, and anxiety neurosis, each with its own psychic characteristics and dynamics.

Freud postulated that neurotic symptoms are manifestations of unresolved psychic conflicts, usually rooted in traumatic experiences or unacceptable desires that have been repressed in the unconscious. These conflicts generate an emotional tension that, without adequate resolution, finds expression through physical or behavioral symptoms. Psychoanalytic therapy seeks to bring these conflicts to consciousness, allowing the patient to confront and integrate them in a healthy way, which often results in the reduction or elimination of symptoms.

One of the most emblematic cases studied by Freud is that of Anna O., pseudonym of Bertha Pappenheim, a young woman who suffered from a series of disabling physical and emotional symptoms, including paralysis, visual and auditory disturbances, and hallucinations. Through the "talking cure" technique, developed by Breuer and perfected by Freud, Anna was encouraged to speak freely about her memories and feelings, bringing to the surface the emotional conflicts underlying her symptoms. This case not only illustrated the effectiveness of the psychoanalytic approach, but also highlighted the importance of verbal and emotional expression in resolving neurotic symptoms.

Another notable case is that of Dora, an 18-year-old girl who had symptoms of hysteria, including loss of voice and chronic cough. Through the analysis of dreams and the exploration of family and emotional conflicts, Freud discovered that Dora's symptoms were linked to a complex love triangle involving her parents and close friends. The therapy helped Dora understand and express her repressed feelings, resulting in a significant improvement of her symptoms.

Freud also investigated obsessive-compulsive neurosis through the famous case of the "Rat Man," a young lawyer who suffered from obsessive thoughts and compulsive rituals.

Freud interpreted these symptoms as attempts to control the anxiety generated by unconscious desires and fears, particularly related to Oedipal conflicts and emotional ambivalence. Therapy focused on exploring and interpreting these conflicts, allowing the patient to develop a deeper understanding of their internal dynamics and thus reduce their symptoms.

These case studies, among many others, form the basis of psychoanalytic theories on neurosis. They illustrate how neurotic symptoms are often rooted in deep emotional experiences and how psychoanalysis can offer an avenue for understanding and resolving these conflicts. Through the analysis of dreams, free association, and the exploration of resistances, psychoanalysis seeks to unearth repressed desires and fears, allowing the patient to integrate these experiences in a healthy and productive way.

Freud's legacy in the study of neuroses is immense and continues to influence contemporary psychology and psychotherapy. His theories on the unconscious, defense mechanisms, and the dynamics of repressed desires offer a powerful framework for understanding the complexity of the human mind. While many of Freud's ideas have been revised and expanded by subsequent generations of psychoanalysts, the fundamental principles he established continue to be a vital part of clinical practice and psychological research.

This book, by exploring the various forms of neurosis through the lens of psychoanalysis, offers the reader a deep and detailed understanding of the emotional and psychological dynamics that shape these disorders. Each chapter is a journey into the inner world of patients, revealing the complexities and challenges they face and how psychoanalysis can help unravel and transform them.

We hope that by the end of this reading, you will not only gain a better understanding of neuroses and psychoanalysis, but also gain a deeper appreciation of the human condition. The human mind, with all its nuances and mysteries, is an inexhaustible field of study and reflection. Psychoanalysis, with its focus on exploring the unconscious and understanding emotional conflicts, offers a unique window into this inner world, providing valuable insights and avenues for healing and growth.

This prologue serves as an invitation to embark on this journey of discovery and understanding. Through the eyes of Freud and his patients, we will be guided into the depths of the unconscious, exploring the labyrinths of the human mind and emerging with a richer and fuller understanding of neuroses and the vital role that psychoanalysis plays in resolving them. May this reading be thought-provoking, enlightening and, above all, a source of inspiration for all who seek to better understand themselves and others.

Psychoanalysis, since its inception by Sigmund Freud in the late nineteenth century, has been a fascinating and controversial field of study and therapeutic practice. This book sets out to explore psychoanalysis through a specific lens: neurosis. Neurosis, a term encompassing a variety of psychological disorders, was one of Freud's main areas of interest, and his theories on the subject have profoundly influenced the modern understanding of the human mind.

The work is organized into chapters that address different forms of neurosis, each analyzed through the psychoanalytic concepts developed by Freud and his followers. Each chapter is enriched with clinical examples taken directly from Freud's texts, providing a practical and applied view of his theories. This book is not only a historical review of Freud's contributions, but also a reflection on how his ideas continue to be relevant and applicable in contemporary clinical practice.

Psychoanalysis, with its deep explorations of the unconscious, defense mechanisms, and the dynamics of repressed desires and fears, offers a unique understanding of neuroses. Understanding these conditions not only illuminates aspects of psychopathology but also reveals much about the human condition in general. Through classic case studies, such as those of Anna O., Dora, and others, the reader is invited on a journey that explores the intricacies of the human psyche, the internal conflicts, and the defense strategies that shape our behavior and emotional experiences.

Part 1: Historical and Theoretical Foundations

Chapter 1: The Origin of Psychoanalysis

Psychoanalysis, one of the most influential approaches to understanding the human mind and behavior, emerged in the late nineteenth century with the groundbreaking works of Sigmund Freud. This chapter explores the historical origins of psychoanalysis, highlighting the key milestones and influences that led to the development of this innovative approach to understanding the human mind.

Emergence of Psychoanalysis

Psychoanalysis was born out of Freud's clinical observations and his attempts to treat mental disorders, particularly hysteria. Influenced by figures such as Jean-Martin Charcot and Josef Breuer, Freud began to investigate the unconscious mind through hypnosis and later the method of free association.

Early Influences and Collaborations

Freud began his medical career in a context where the understanding of mental disorders was rudimentary. During his studies in Paris with Jean-Martin Charcot, Freud was exposed to the use of hypnosis in the treatment of hysteria. Charcot demonstrated that hysterical symptoms could be induced and removed through hypnosis, suggesting a psychological basis for these disorders. This experience profoundly influenced Freud, leading him to explore the unconscious as an explanation for the unexplained mental and physical symptoms.

Back in Vienna, Freud began to collaborate with Josef Breuer. Together, they developed the "cathartic method," which consisted of inducing patients to recall and verbalize repressed traumatic memories, often resulting in symptom relief. This approach was detailed in the book "Studies on Hysteria" (1895), co-written by Freud and Breuer. This work marked the formal beginning of psychoanalysis and highlighted the importance of unconscious processes in the genesis of neurotic symptoms.

The Case of Anna O.

Anna O., pseudonym of Bertha Pappenheim, was a patient treated by Breuer between 1880 and 1882. She had a range of symptoms, including paralysis, visual and hearing disturbances, and episodes of loss of consciousness. Breuer and Freud found that by recalling traumatic events in a hypnotic state, Anna O. experienced temporary relief from her symptoms. Freud interpreted this as evidence that hysterical symptoms were symbolic expressions of repressed psychic conflicts.

Anna O. was crucial to the development of hysteria theory and the cathartic method. Freud saw in this case proof that neurotic symptoms could be treated by bringing repressed traumas to consciousness. This insight was fundamental to the formulation of the technique of free association and dream analysis.

Freud and the Development of Early Theories

Over the next few years, Freud continued to develop and refine his theories. He moved away from hypnosis and began using "free association," where patients were encouraged to speak freely whatever came to mind, without censorship. This method has turned out to be a powerful tool for accessing the unconscious.

The Interpretation of Dreams

In 1900, Freud published "The Interpretation of Dreams," a foundational work that introduced the theory that dreams are the disguised fulfillment of repressed desires. He proposed that dreams have a manifest content (the dream as remembered by the dreamer) and a latent content (the unconscious desires and thoughts that the dream represents). This work laid the foundation for the analysis of unconscious processes and is considered a milestone in the history of psychoanalysis.

Freud described dreams as the "royal way" to the unconscious, an idea that allowed for the exploration of deep aspects of the human psyche. The book introduced concepts such as dream censorship and condensation, mechanisms by which repressed contents are transformed into dream images.

Early Theories of Child Sexuality

Another crucial point in the development of psychoanalysis was the introduction of the theory of infantile sexuality. In works such as "Three Essays on the Theory of Sexuality" (1905), Freud argued that sexuality does not begin at puberty, but is present from birth and goes through several stages of development: oral, anal, phallic, latency, and genital. Each phase is associated with different erogenous zones and psychic conflicts.

The idea that adult neurosis could be traced back to the unresolved conflicts of these childhood phases was revolutionary. Freud postulated that sexual desires repressed during childhood could manifest in neurotic symptoms in adulthood. This concept challenged contemporary notions of morality and human development, but provided a basis for understanding many psychic disorders.

The Hysteria Studies

Hysteria studies played a crucial role in shaping Freud's ideas. Hysteria was a common diagnosis at the time, characterized by physical symptoms with no apparent organic cause, such as paralysis, seizures, and blindness. Freud and Breuer treated several cases of hysteria using the cathartic method, including the famous case of Anna O.

The Case of Dora

Freud continued to investigate cases of hysteria and other neurotic disorders, refining his techniques and theories. The case of "Dora" (Ida Bauer), a young woman with hysterical symptoms, was documented in "Fragment of an Analysis of a Case of Hysteria" (1905). Dora showed symptoms such as breathing difficulties, nervous cough, and loss of voice, which Freud interpreted as expressions of unresolved psychic conflicts.

Freud associated Dora's symptoms with repressed sexual conflicts, particularly related to desire for her father and jealousy of her father's mistress. This case allowed Freud to elaborate his ideas on transference, where unconscious feelings are projected onto the analyst, and the importance of interpersonal relationships in the formation of neurotic symptoms.

The Case of the Rat Man

Another famous case study is that of Ernst Lanzer, known as "The Rat Man", described by Freud in "Notes on a Case of Obsessional Neurosis" (1909). Lanzer suffered from obsessive thoughts about torture involving rats, accompanied by compulsive rituals to relieve anxiety. Freud identified these symptoms as symbolic expressions of unconscious conflicts related to repressed desires for aggression and sexuality.

This case exemplified the theory that obsessive-compulsive symptoms result from trying to control unacceptable desires through ritualistic thoughts and behaviors. The analysis revealed how Lanzer used compulsive rituals to avoid the distress associated with his unconscious desires.

The Case of Little Hans

Hans's study, described in "Analysis of a Phobia in a Five-Year-Old Boy" (1909), is one of the most famous examples of childhood phobia. Hans developed a phobia of horses, which Freud interpreted as a symbolic manifestation of Oedipal conflicts. Hans was afraid of being bitten by a horse, which Freud associated with the fear of castration and the unconscious desire to replace his father as the object of his mother's love.

This case demonstrated the application of psychoanalytic theories to child development and the importance of resolving oedipal conflicts for healthy psychic development.

The origin of psychoanalysis is rooted in Freud's pioneering efforts to understand and treat mental disorders through the exploration of the unconscious. His early collaborations with Breuer, influences from Charcot, and the development of techniques such as free association and dream analysis were instrumental in the establishment of psychoanalysis. The classic case studies of hysteria and other neurotic disorders have provided valuable insights into the human mind and paved the way for a new therapeutic approach.

Freud not only founded psychoanalysis, but also provided a new understanding of human nature, challenging contemporary conceptions and ushering in a revolution in the treatment of mental disorders. This chapter only scratches the surface of Freud's vast legacy, which will be explored in more detail in subsequent chapters of this book. Understanding these origins is critical to appreciating the complexity and depth of psychoanalytic theory and practice.

Chapter 2: Defining Neurosis

What is Neurosis?

Neurosis, one of the central concepts in psychoanalysis, is a complex psychological condition characterized by internal conflicts that result in anxiety and defensive behaviors. Sigmund Freud, the founder of psychoanalysis, defined neurosis as a mental disorder that emerges from the repression of unconscious desires. These desires, when repressed, generate neurotic symptoms that can manifest themselves in various ways, such as obsessions, compulsions, phobias, and physical symptoms without a clear organic cause.

Neurosis is essentially a conflict between unconscious desires and the ego's defense mechanisms. When these desires are repressed by the ego as being deemed unacceptable or threatening, they become inaccessible to consciousness. However, these repressed desires continue to influence the individual's behavior and emotional state, resulting in neurotic symptoms.

Examples and References

The classic example is the case of Anna O., treated by Freud and Josef Breuer, described in "Studies on Hysteria" (1895). Anna O. exhibited hysterical symptoms such as paralysis and hallucinations, which were interpreted as symbolic manifestations of repressed emotional conflicts. A classic case, again "The Rat Man," of Freud's patient who suffered from obsessive-compulsive neurosis. Their obsessive symptoms and ritualistic compulsions were expressions of repressed unconscious desires and inner conflicts.

Freud details the dynamics of neurosis in several of his works, including "Three Essays on the Theory of Sexuality" (1905) and "The Interpretation of Dreams" (1900). In these texts, he explores how repressed desires, particularly those of a sexual nature, are channeled into the unconscious, resulting in neurotic manifestations.

Difference Between Neurosis, Psychosis, and Perversion

Psychoanalysis clearly distinguishes between neurosis, psychosis, and perversion, each representing different modes of mental functioning and relationship to reality.

Neurosis

Neurosis is characterized by a conflict between the ego and the id, where the ego tries to control the id's impulses through defense mechanisms. Neurotic individuals maintain a touch with reality, although their perceptions and behaviors may be distorted by anxiety and unconscious conflicts.

Psychosis

Psychosis, in contrast, involves a break with reality. In psychosis, the ego cannot properly mediate between external reality and the impulses of the id, resulting in delusions and hallucinations. Freud explored psychosis in texts such as "Psychoanalytic Notes on an Autobiographical Account of a Case of Paranoia" (1911), where he analyzed the case of Schreber, a judge who suffered from paranoia and believed he was transforming himself into a woman as part of a divine plan.

Perversion

Perversion is related to a fixation on deviant forms of sexual gratification, deviating from cultural norms. Freud discusses perversion in "Three Essays on the Theory of Sexuality," where he identifies various forms of perverse sexual behavior that, according to him, are manifestations of fixations at early stages of sexual development.

Psychoanalytic View of Neurosis

The psychoanalytic view of neurosis is that it results from the repression of unconscious desires. Freud saw neurotic symptoms as symbolic manifestations of these repressed conflicts. He believed that psychoanalytic therapy could bring these conflicts into consciousness, allowing the individual to understand and resolve their neurotic anxieties and behaviors.

Defense Mechanisms

Defense mechanisms are unconscious processes that the ego uses to protect itself from anxiety caused by internal conflicts. Freud, and later his daughter Anna Freud, identified various defense mechanisms, including repression, denial, projection, rationalization, and displacement.

- **Repression**: Keeping unacceptable desires and memories out of consciousness.
- **Denial**: Refusing to accept the reality of a painful situation.
- **Projection**: Attributing one's own unacceptable desires to other people.
- **Rationalization**: Justifying behaviors or feelings with logical but false reasons.

- **Displacement**: Transferring feelings or impulses from a threatening object to a less threatening object.

Examples of Clinical Cases

Freud illustrated these concepts with several clinical cases. In "Analysis of a Phobia in a Five-Year-Old Boy" (1909), known as the case of "Little Hans," Freud described the boy's phobia of horses as a symbolic manifestation of his Oedipal conflicts. Hans's analysis revealed how anxiety resulting from repressed desires toward parents was shifted to horses, a more manageable external object.

Another example is the case of "Dora," described in "Fragment of the Analysis of a Case of Hysteria" (1905). Dora, a young woman with hysterical symptoms, exhibited a series of physical and emotional symptoms that Freud interpreted as expressions of repressed sexual desires and conflicts.

Neurosis, from the psychoanalytic perspective, is a complex condition resulting from unconscious conflicts between repressed desires and defense mechanisms. The distinction between neurosis, psychosis, and perversion is crucial for understanding mental dynamics and appropriate therapeutic approaches. Through the analysis of clinical cases and the exploration of defense mechanisms, psychoanalysis seeks to bring to light repressed conflicts, providing an opportunity for resolution and healing for individuals suffering from neuroses.

Chapter 3: Main Psychoanalytic Concepts Related to Neurosis

To understand neurosis deeply and comprehensively, it is essential to become familiar with the fundamental concepts of psychoanalysis. Sigmund Freud, the father of psychoanalysis, developed a number of theories and concepts that form the basis for understanding neurotic processes. This chapter explores in detail the notions of the unconscious, repression, resistance, psychic conflict, and defense mechanisms, offering clinical examples and references to classic Freud cases.

Unconscious, Preconscious, and Conscious

Freud postulated that the human mind is structured on three distinct levels: unconscious, preconscious, and conscious. This division is crucial for understanding the psychic processes that lead to the formation of neuroses.

Unconscious

The unconscious is the deepest part of the mind, where repressed desires, memories, and experiences reside. These contents are kept out of consciousness because they are considered unacceptable or threatening. Freud argued that the unconscious exerts a powerful influence on conscious behavior and thoughts, even if the individual is not aware of it.

Clinical Example: A patient who exhibits an irrational fear of water may have repressed a traumatic memory of near-drowning in childhood. This memory, held in the unconscious, influences your current behavior.

Reference: In "The Interpretation of Dreams" (1900), Freud describes how dreams are a way of access to the unconscious, revealing repressed desires and conflicts.

Pre-conscious

The preconscious is the intermediate level of the mind. It contains thoughts and memories that are not immediately accessible to consciousness, but can be brought to the surface with some effort. The preconscious serves as a filter between the unconscious and the conscious, regulating the flow of information.

Clinical Example: During a therapy session, a patient may initially not remember a specific event, but by being encouraged to speak freely, they can bring this memory from the preconscious into consciousness.

Reference: Freud explores the preconscious in the context of the technique of free association, as described in "Studies on Hysteria" (1895).

Conscious

The conscious mind is the part of the mind responsible for immediate perception and rational thought. It involves everything we are aware of at any given moment, including thoughts, feelings, and sensory perceptions.

Clinical Example: A patient consciously reports his or her difficulties at work, without initially understanding that these difficulties may be linked to unconscious conflicts.

Reference: Freud discusses the structure of the mind in "The Ego and the Id" (1923), where he describes the dynamics between the different levels of consciousness.

Repression and Resistance

Repression and resistance are central psychic mechanisms in Freud's theory of neurosis. Both play crucial roles in the way the unconscious influences neurotic behavior and symptoms.

Repression

Repression is the process by which unacceptable desires and memories are excluded from consciousness and relegated to the unconscious. This defense mechanism is fundamental for psychic functioning, but when excessive, it can lead to the development of neurotic symptoms.

Clinical Example: A woman who represses feelings of anger toward her father may develop symptoms of depression, as these repressed feelings find other forms of expression.

Reference: In the case of "Anna O." described in "Studies on Hysteria" (1895), Freud and Breuer note how the repression of intense emotions resulted in physical symptoms of hysteria.

Resistance

Resistance is the force that prevents repressed content from coming to the surface during therapy. During psychoanalytic treatment, patients often show resistance when recalling or talking about painful memories, a defense mechanism to avoid the anxiety associated with these contents.

Clinical Example: A patient may change the subject or forget therapeutic commitments when therapy approaches emotionally charged topics.

Reference: Freud explores resistance in "Remembering, Repeating, and Elaborating" (1914), where he discusses how resistance can manifest itself and how it should be addressed in therapy.

Psychic Conflict and Defense

Neurosis results from psychic conflicts between instinctive impulses and defense mechanisms. These conflicts generate anxiety, which is mitigated by defenses such as repression, denial, and projection. Understanding this dynamic is essential for the analysis and treatment of neurosis.

Psychic Conflict

Psychic conflicts arise when instinctual desires or impulses (usually coming from the id) clash with the demands of reality or with internalized values (superego). These conflicts generate anxiety, which the ego tries to manage through various defense mechanisms.

Clinical Example: A man who is attracted to his co-worker (desire of the id) may feel guilty due to his moral beliefs and loyalty to his wife (superego), resulting in anxiety and defensive behaviors.

Reference: In "Beyond the Pleasure Principle" (1920), Freud discusses how psychic conflicts can lead to compulsive repetition and symptom formation.

Defense Mechanisms

Defense mechanisms are unconscious strategies used by the ego to protect itself from the anxiety generated by psychic conflicts. They distort reality in some way to relieve tension and preserve psychic functioning.

Main Defense Mechanisms:

1. **Repression:** Exclusion of unacceptable thoughts and desires from consciousness.
    - **Clinical Example:** A man who represses memories of childhood abuse may develop partial amnesia for certain periods of his life.
2. **Denial:** Refusal to accept the reality of a painful situation.
    - **Clinical Example:** A woman diagnosed with a terminal illness may deny the severity of her condition by acting as if she is healthy.
3. **Projection:** Attribution of unacceptable desires or feelings of oneself to another person.
    - **Clinical Example:** A man with feelings of hostility may believe that others are hostile toward him.
4. **Rationalization:** Logical or socially acceptable justification for behaviors or feelings that are, in fact, driven by unconscious motives.
    - **Clinical Example:** A student who fails an exam may rationalize by saying that the test

was not important, when in fact they fear failure.
5. **Displacement:** Transference of feelings from a threatening object to a safer substitute.
    - **Clinical Example:** An employee who is frustrated with his boss may take out his anger on his family.

Reference: Freud discusses defense mechanisms extensively in "The Ego and the Defense Mechanisms" (1936), a work expanded upon by his daughter Anna Freud.

Chapter 4: Anxiety Neurosis

Anxiety neurosis is one of the most common forms of neurosis, characterized by an intense and persistent feeling of anxiety that has no apparent or proportionate cause. This chapter explores in depth the characteristics, causes, and psychoanalytic treatments of anxiety neurosis, enriching the discussion with clinical examples and references to classic cases treated by Sigmund Freud.

Characteristics and Symptoms of Anxiety Neurosis

Anxiety neurosis is defined by a range of symptoms that include excessive worry, muscle tension, palpitations, sweating, shaking, and a constant feeling of fear or apprehension. These symptoms can be generalized or specific to certain situations or objects. Unlike phobias, anxiety neurosis is not necessarily linked to a specific stimulus, which makes identification and treatment more complex.

Common Symptoms

1. **Excessive Worry:** Individuals with anxiety neurosis often worry excessively and irrationally about everyday issues. This worry is disproportionate to the reality of the situations and can consume a significant amount of time and mental energy.

    Clinical Example: A woman may be obsessively worried that she will lose her job, even though she is performing excellently and there are no real indications that she will be fired.

2. **Physical Symptoms:** Anxiety manifests itself physically through muscle tension, headaches, nausea, sweating, tremors, and palpitations. These physical symptoms are a result of activation of the autonomic nervous system, particularly the sympathetic system.

    Clinical Example: A man may experience palpitations and heavy sweating whenever he has to speak in public, even in informal situations.

3. **Constant Fear:** The feeling of fear or apprehension is always present, even if there is no clear reason. This fear can be related to a variety of situations, or it can be a generalized feeling without a specific focus.

    Clinical Example: A person may feel a constant fear that something bad will happen at any moment, without being able to identify a specific cause for that fear.

Differentiation from Other Disorders

It is important to differentiate anxiety neurosis from other anxiety disorders, such as panic disorder, generalized anxiety disorder (GAD), and specific phobias. Anxiety neurosis, as defined by Freud, involves an underlying psychic conflict and defense mechanisms, while other disorders may have multifactorial causes including biological, cognitive, and behavioral components.

Reference: Freud addresses anxiety neurosis in several of his texts, including "Inhibitions, Symptoms, and Anxiety" (1926), where he discusses the relationship between anxiety and repression.

Causes and Mechanisms of Anxiety Neurosis

Psychoanalysis sees anxiety neurosis as resulting from unconscious conflicts and repressed traumatic experiences. Defense mechanisms, such as the repression of painful memories, play a crucial role in the etiology of this condition. These unconscious conflicts and traumas generate an internal tension that manifests as anxiety.

Unconscious Conflicts

Freud postulated that anxiety neurosis is often linked to unconscious conflicts involving repressed desires, fears, and trauma. These conflicts generate a psychic energy that, if not properly channeled or resolved, manifests as anxiety.

Clinical Example: A patient who has experienced emotional abuse in childhood may repress these painful memories. The conflict between the need to express these pent-up emotions and the fear of confronting the pain associated with trauma can generate constant anxiety.

Reference: In the case of the "Rat Man," Freud observed that the patient's obsessive thoughts and compulsions were linked to unconscious conflicts involving repressed sadistic desires and guilt.

Defense Mechanisms

Defense mechanisms, such as repression, denial, and projection, are used by the ego to manage the anxiety generated by unconscious conflicts. Although these mechanisms are effective in the short term, their overuse can lead to the development of neurotic symptoms.

1. **Repression:** The process of keeping unacceptable thoughts and desires out of consciousness. While repression helps protect the individual from immediate anxiety, it also prevents the resolution of the underlying conflicts.

    Clinical Example: An individual who represses their fear of failure may develop generalized anxiety as the psychic energy associated with fear is not adequately expressed or resolved.

2. **Projection:** Attributing one's own feelings or desires to another person. This mechanism allows the individual to deal with unacceptable feelings without acknowledging them as their own.

Clinical Example: A person who feels inadequate may project these feelings onto co-workers, believing that they judge or look down on them.

In "The Ego and Defense Mechanisms" (1936), Anna Freud expands on her father's ideas about how defense mechanisms operate and contribute to the formation of neurotic symptoms.

Psychoanalytic Treatment of Anxiety Neurosis

Psychoanalytic treatment of anxiety neurosis involves bringing to awareness the repressed conflicts and resolving the underlying traumas. Psychoanalytic techniques, such as free association and dream interpretation, are fundamental in this process.

Free Membership

Free association is a central technique in psychoanalysis, where the patient is encouraged to speak freely about any thought or feeling that comes to mind. This process allows unconscious content to emerge and be analyzed.

Clinical Example: A patient with anxiety may initially talk about their everyday concerns. Over time, through free association, he can reveal repressed memories of childhood traumas that are at the root of his anxiety.

Reference: Freud details the technique of free association in "On Psychotherapy" (1905), explaining how it can help unveil the unconscious.

Dream Interpretation

Dreams are seen by Freud as the "royal way" to the unconscious. Dream interpretation involves analyzing the manifest content (what is remembered from the dream) and the latent content (the hidden meanings and repressed desires).

Clinical Example: A patient with anxiety neurosis may report a recurring dream of being lost in an unfamiliar place. Analysis of this dream may reveal a deep-seated fear of helplessness or abandonment, linked to past experiences.

Reference: In "The Interpretation of Dreams" (1900), Freud describes how dreams are expressions of repressed desires and unconscious conflicts, offering valuable insights for therapy.

Transfer Job

Transference is the process by which patients project feelings and attitudes toward important figures from their past (such as parents) onto the therapist. Analyzing and resolving these transferential feelings is crucial for treatment.

Clinical Example: A patient who has transferred feelings of fear and distrust from the father to the therapist can, through the analysis of this transference, understand the source of their anxiety and work through these feelings.

Reference: Freud discusses the importance of transference and countertransference in "On the Dynamics of Transference" (1912), where he highlights how these processes can be used therapeutically to reveal and resolve unconscious conflicts.

Chapter 5: Obsessive-Compulsive Neurosis

Obsessive-compulsive neurosis (NOC) is a psychological condition characterized by the presence of obsessions — intrusive and unwanted thoughts — and compulsions — repetitive behaviors performed to relieve the anxiety generated by obsessions. This chapter explores in detail its clinical manifestations, the underlying psychic dynamics, a classic case study, and the therapeutic approach from a psychoanalytic perspective.

Symptomatology and Psychic Dynamics

The symptoms of obsessive-compulsive neurosis are widely recognized in clinical psychopathology. Obsessions can take many forms, from thoughts of contamination to fears of unintentionally causing harm to others. For example, an individual may suffer from an intense obsession with cleanliness, fearing contamination by germs, which leads to compulsive rituals of handwashing multiple times a day. Other examples include repeatedly checking to see if doors are locked or compulsively counting objects.

Freud deeply explored the psychic dynamics behind these symptoms, arguing that obsessions and compulsions are defense mechanisms against repressed internal conflicts. He postulated that obsessive thoughts are often symbolic manifestations of unacceptable or traumatic desires that have been repressed into the unconscious. Compulsions, in turn, serve as a way to counteract the anxiety associated with these intrusive thoughts.

Freud described obsessions as "substitutive representatives" of repressed impulses and desires. These intrusive thoughts are disguised ways in which unconscious and often disturbing desires try to emerge into consciousness. The binge, then, acts as an attempt at mitigation, a ritual that, while irrational, offers a temporary sense of relief or control over the anxiety brought on by the obsessive thoughts.

Case Study: "The Rat Man"

One of Freud's most iconic case studies is that of "The Rat Man" (Ernst Lanzer), which offers a rich illustration of the complexity of obsessive-compulsive neurosis. Lanzer was intensely obsessed with the idea that something terrible would happen to his father or those close to him if he didn't perform specific protective rituals. For example, he felt compelled to count in a specific sequence or touch objects in a ritualistic manner to avert an impending catastrophe.

Freud interpreted these obsessions as symbolic expressions of repressed desires and deep emotional conflicts, often rooted in childhood experiences and complex family relationships. In the case of the Rat Man, obsessions with his father's safety were a way of dealing with unconscious desires for aggression or resentment towards his father. Compulsions functioned as attempts to prevent these repressed desires from coming to fruition in reality.

Freud revealed that Lanzer had a disturbing fantasy involving a cruel method of torture he had heard during his military service, in which rats were introduced into the victim's anus. This fantasy was associated with feelings of guilt and punishment, reflecting deep-rooted Oedipal conflicts and an intense ambivalence towards father figures.

Therapeutic Approach

Psychoanalytic therapy of obsessive-compulsive neurosis focuses on bringing to consciousness the underlying emotional conflicts and unconscious desires that fuel the obsessions and compulsions. The therapeutic techniques employed include free association, where the patient is encouraged to freely report their thoughts and feelings, allowing unconscious contents to surface.

Dream interpretation also plays a key role in psychoanalytic therapy, helping to reveal repressed contents that manifest in a symbolic way during sleep. Dreams, according to Freud, are the "royal highway to the unconscious," offering valuable insights into the inner conflicts that contribute to neurotic symptoms. For example, dreams involving themes of dirt or persecution may reflect hidden fears and desires that manifest in the patient's obsessions and compulsions.

In addition, the analysis of resistances is essential to identify and work through the psychic defenses that keep repressed contents away from consciousness. Resistances are defense mechanisms that arise during the therapeutic process to prevent the patient from coming into contact with emotionally painful or disturbing content. Freud highlighted the importance of recognizing and interpreting these resistances as a way to unblock repressed traumas and desires.

Detailed Examples of Overcoming in Therapy

Let's consider some more detailed fictional examples to illustrate how psychoanalytic therapy can help NOC patients overcome their symptoms.

Pedro's Case: Fear of Contamination

Pedro, a fictional patient, suffered from an intense obsession with cleanliness, fearing contamination by germs to the point of washing his hands until his skin was raw. During therapy, through the technique of free association, Pedro began to relate childhood memories where his mother severely scolded him for playing in the mud, associating dirt with guilt and punishment. Freud would interpret this as an Oedipal conflict shifted to the obsession with cleanliness.

By tapping into these pent-up feelings, Peter was able to recognize that his obsession with cleanliness was a way of dealing with deep feelings of guilt and the need for self-punishment. As he confronted these emotions and reevaluated his relationship with his mother figure, his compulsive rituals began to subside, being replaced by a new understanding of himself and his emotional needs.

Maria's Case: Compulsion to Check

Maria, another fictitious patient, had a compulsion to repeatedly check that the doors were locked, which caused her to spend hours each night performing this task. Through psychoanalytic therapy, it became clear that Maria had a deep-seated fear of invasion that harkened back to an unstable childhood where her parents often argued violently, making her feel unsafe in her own home.

The interpretation of Maria's dreams, which often involved intruders or break-ins, helped reveal her unconscious fear of loss of control and security. Over time, as she worked through these feelings of insecurity and confronted the painful memories of her childhood, Maria began to realize that her compulsions were an attempt to regain a sense of control. The therapy helped her develop new coping mechanisms, gradually reducing her checking compulsions.

John's Case: Aggressive Obsessions

John, a fictitious third patient, suffered from aggressive obsessions, fearing that he might unintentionally hurt loved ones. During therapy, John revealed that in his childhood, he often felt intense anger towards his younger brother, but these emotions were suppressed due to his parents' severe reprimands.

Through free association, John began to understand that his aggressive obsessions were manifestations of these repressed feelings of anger and brotherly rivalry. The compulsions to avoid situations where he might be near sharp or potentially dangerous objects were actually attempts to suppress these unacceptable emotions. By working through these conflicts and allowing himself to feel and express his anger in a healthy way, John was able to significantly decrease his obsessions and compulsions.

Integration with Other Therapeutic Approaches

While psychoanalysis offers unparalleled depth in understanding unconscious conflicts, the integration of other therapeutic approaches can complement this perspective by offering practical strategies for dealing with symptoms.

Cognitive Behavioral Therapy (CBT), for example, can be integrated with psychoanalysis to help patients modify dysfunctional thoughts and maladaptive behaviors. CBT techniques, such as exposure with response prevention, can be used in conjunction with psychoanalytic exploration to provide immediate symptomatic relief while unconscious conflicts are worked through.

Laura's Case: Integration of CBT and Psychoanalysis

Laura, a fictional patient with NOC, benefited from the combination of CBT and psychoanalysis. While CBT helped Laura directly confront her checking compulsions through exposure techniques, psychoanalysis allowed her to explore the unconscious roots of her fear of failure and being punished, which went back to an extremely rigid upbringing.

By combining these approaches, Laura was not only able to reduce her compulsive behaviors but also developed a deeper understanding of her underlying fears, promoting lasting change in her emotional life.

Obsessive-compulsive neurosis, with its complex clinical manifestations and deep-rooted psychic dynamics, vividly illustrates the fundamental principles of Freud's psychoanalytic theory. By interpreting symptoms not only as superficial manifestations but as symbolic expressions of unconscious conflicts and desires, psychoanalytic therapy offers a path to lasting symptom resolution. Understanding and treating NOC not only relieves the patient's anxiety but also promotes deeper psychic integration and greater emotional well-being.

The analysis of the Rat Man case exemplifies how psychoanalysis can elucidate the origins and dynamics underlying obsessive-compulsive neuroses, offering valuable perspectives for mental health professionals seeking to understand and help individuals suffering from these complex symptoms. In addition, it highlights the importance of a therapeutic approach that goes beyond the mere suppression of symptoms, aiming at a deep understanding and resolution of the internal conflicts that give rise to obsessive-compulsive neurosis.

The future of psychoanalysis in the treatment of NOC promises a more integrated and flexible approach, incorporating insights from diverse disciplines to deliver a more holistic and effective treatment. By continuing to explore and integrate new therapeutic approaches, psychoanalysis reaffirms its relevance and effectiveness in understanding and treating the psychic complexities that characterize NOC, helping patients achieve a more balanced and satisfying life.

Chapter 6: Hysteria

Hysteria is one of the most intriguing forms of neurosis studied in the early days of psychoanalysis, characterized by physical symptoms without an identifiable organic cause. This chapter explores in depth its clinical manifestations, its psychological roots according to Freud, and a classic case study to illustrate the theoretical and therapeutic principles of psychoanalysis.

Clinical Manifestation

Hysteria manifests itself through physical symptoms that have no clear physiological basis, such as paralysis, hysterical blindness, seizures, and other unexplained somatic phenomena. These symptoms often arise in response to deep-seated psychological conflicts and can vary widely between patients.

For example, in "Studies on Hysteria," Freud and Breuer reported cases of patients who had paralysis in one part of the body as a result of unresolved emotional trauma. A famous case is that of Anna O., a patient who developed several disabling physical symptoms, including partial paralysis, visual and hearing disturbances, and vivid hallucinations.

Symptoms and Interpretation

Anna O.'s symptoms were diverse and striking. She suffered from partial paralysis that affected her ability to use her right arm and legs, visual and hearing disturbances that included periods of temporary blindness and deafness, and vivid hallucinations during states of hypnosis or semi-hypnosis. In addition, Anna experienced loss of speech, often speaking only in English despite being German.

Breuer and Freud interpreted Anna's persistent cough as a reaction to an episode in which she cared for her seriously ill father, whose illness involved breathing problems. By bringing these memories and the associated repressed emotions to consciousness, Anna experienced a significant reduction in her physical symptoms. For example, the partial paralysis of Anna's right arm has been linked to an experience in which she was holding her father's arm as he was dying. As he recalled and worked through this memory, the function of his arm gradually returned.

Another notable example was the hallucination of a snake that Anna had while standing at her father's bedside. Breuer interpreted this hallucination as a symbolic representation of his fear and anxiety regarding his father's death. By talking about this hallucination and exploring her underlying emotions, Anna was able to reduce her anxiety and, subsequently, the hallucinatory episodes.

Psychoanalytic Interpretation

In psychoanalysis, hysterical symptoms are seen as a conversion of emotional conflicts and repressed desires into physical symptoms. Freud argued that these somatic symptoms represent an attempt by the individual to unconsciously express their inner conflicts, often in a symbolic form that can be decoded through psychoanalytic interpretation.

Freud and Breuer proposed that hysterical symptoms were physical manifestations of repressed memories of traumatic events and that speech and emotional expression could bring these memories to consciousness and alleviate symptoms. In Anna O.'s case, arm paralysis was associated with the traumatic experience of holding her dying father's arm. The therapy focused on bringing these memories to the surface and processing them emotionally, which led to remission of the symptoms.

Case Study: Dora

Another classic case study is that of Dora, an 18-year-old who experienced a range of hysterical symptoms, including loss of voice and chronic cough. Freud discovered that Dora's symptoms were related to complex emotional conflicts involving her family and a complex love triangle between her parents and their close friends.

Dora's cough, for example, was interpreted by Freud as a hysterical symptom related to a traumatic episode in which she witnessed a scene of sexual intimacy between her father and a family friend, Mrs. K. Throughout therapy, Freud helped Dora explore and understand these traumatic experiences and the associated repressed feelings, which resulted in a reduction in her symptoms.

Freud also associated Dora's loss of voice with her feeling of not being able to express her true desires and frustrations, especially regarding her father's behavior and her interactions with Mr. K. By allowing Dora to express these feelings in a safe environment, therapy helped alleviate the loss of voice and other symptoms.

Therapeutic Approach

Psychoanalytic hysteria therapy aims to explore and resolve the underlying unconscious conflicts that are being converted into physical symptoms. Techniques such as free association, dream interpretation, and resistance analysis are essential in this therapeutic process. Free association allows the patient to freely explore his or her mental associations, bringing to the surface unconscious contents that contribute to hysterical symptoms.

Dream interpretation plays a significant role in hysteria therapy, since dreams are seen as symbolic expressions of the patient's unconscious desires and conflicts. By analyzing dreams, the therapist can uncover hidden connections between physical symptoms and emotional events in the patient's life, making it easier to understand and resolve the underlying conflicts.

In addition, the analysis of resistances – the defense mechanisms that arise to prevent the patient from coming into contact with painful emotional content – is crucial. Freud believed that bringing these contents to consciousness and working through resistances would allow the patient to integrate these experiences in a healthy way, thus reducing the need for conversion into physical symptoms.

Classic Examples of Overcoming in Therapy

Anna O.'s case:

Anna O., whose real name was Bertha Pappenheim, was treated by Breuer and Freud and is one of the most documented cases in "Studies on Hysteria." Her therapy included the "talking healing" technique, where she was encouraged to freely express her thoughts and memories associated with the physical symptoms. Over the course of treatment, Anna experienced a gradual remission of symptoms, such as the recovery of function in her paralyzed arm and a reduction in episodes of blindness and deafness.

Case of Elisabeth von R.:

Another case documented by Freud is that of Elisabeth von R., who suffered from leg pain that prevented her from walking. Freud found that these pains were linked to feelings of guilt and conflict related to his father's death and the unconscious desire to free himself from family responsibilities in order to pursue an independent life. Through the technique of free association, Elisabeth was able to bring out these repressed memories and feelings, resulting in the reduction of pain and the recovery of the ability to walk.

Emmy von N. Case:

Emmy von N. was a patient who experienced a number of hysterical symptoms, including spasms and episodes of terror. Freud used the technique of free association and hypnosis to explore the underlying causes of his symptoms. He found that Emmy's spasms were related to past emotional trauma and unresolved conflicts. By allowing her to express and process these traumas, her symptoms decreased significantly.

Hysteria, with its intriguing clinical manifestations and deep psychological roots, exemplifies the fundamental tenets of Freud's psychoanalysis. By exploring how emotional conflicts are converted into physical symptoms, psychoanalysis offers a deep understanding of neuroses and an avenue to effective treatment. Classic case studies, such as those of Anna O., Dora, Elisabeth von R., and Emmy von N., vividly illustrate how psychoanalytic interpretation can unravel the hidden meanings behind hysterical symptoms, promoting not only symptom remission but also greater psychic integration and emotional well-being.

This chapter offers a comprehensive analysis of hysteria in psychoanalysis, highlighting its clinical relevance and the therapeutic strategies that have evolved since Freud's early studies. By understanding and treating hysteria, mental health professionals can not only alleviate the suffering of patients but also promote a deeper understanding of the mental processes underlying the manifestation of neurotic symptoms. Freud wrote in "Studies on Hysteria" that "the hysteric suffers chiefly from reminiscences"—an observation that underlines the importance of understanding the past events that shape the patient's present experience. Psychoanalysis, with its detailed and empathetic approach, continues to offer valuable insights and effective therapeutic techniques for those suffering from this complex and multifaceted condition.

Chapter 7: Phobias and Phobic Neuroses

Phobias constitute an intriguing field of study in psychoanalysis, characterized by intense and irrational fears of specific objects or situations. This chapter sets out to thoroughly explore the psychoanalytic understanding of phobias, providing a detailed analysis grounded in the principles outlined by Freud and enriched by emblematic case studies and innovative therapeutic strategies.

Understanding Phobia in Psychoanalysis

The psychoanalytic approach to phobias differs in that it is not limited to superficial symptoms, but enters into the unconscious dynamics that give rise to and sustain these pathological manifestations. According to Freud, phobias arise as a way of displacing anxiety from unresolved internal conflicts to a specific external object or situation. This defense mechanism allows the individual to avoid directly confronting the true object of his anguish, symbolically replacing it with something less disturbing.

In psychoanalytic theory, the development of phobias is closely linked to the concept of displaced anxiety. The individual, unable to deal directly with the anxiety caused by an internal conflict, transfers this anxiety to an external object or situation, creating a phobia. This process of displacement allows the person to keep anxiety at bay while avoiding confronting the real underlying conflict.

Case Study: "Little Hans"

One of the classic cases that vividly illustrates this conception is that of "Little Hans", a boy tormented by an intense phobia of horses. Detailed analysis of this case revealed that the phobia was not directly about horses, but rather a symbolic manifestation of deep emotional conflicts related to Oedipal issues. Freud interpreted that the fear of horses represented, in fact, the unconscious fear of the father and the anguish of castration, central themes in Freudian psychoanalytic theory.

Hans, whose real name was Herbert Graf, began to develop his phobia of horses at the age of five. He feared that the horses would bite him or fall on him. The analysis conducted by Freud, with the help of Hans's father, who provided detailed observations and participated in the therapy, led to the interpretation that the phobia of horses was a displacement of his fears and desires related to the Oedipus complex.

Symptoms and Interpretation

Hans manifested specific symptoms that included a paralyzing fear of leaving the house, especially if he saw a horse. This fear was accompanied by intense anxiety and avoidance. By investigating Hans's dreams and fantasies, Freud discovered that the boy was afraid of being bitten by the horses, which he interpreted as a symbolic representation of the fear of castration, linked to the Oedipal conflict.

For example, Hans had a dream where a horse fell and struggled, which Freud interpreted as a symbolic fear of castration and rivalry with his father. Hans's fear of being bitten by a horse was linked to his unconscious fear of being punished by his father for his incestuous desires towards his mother. The analysis revealed that the horse symbolized the father, and Hans's phobia was a way of coping with these complex and distressing feelings.

Therapeutic Process

Hans's treatment involved a series of conversations between the boy and his father, who followed Freud's directions. These conversations were intended to bring Hans's repressed feelings to awareness and help reduce the intensity of his phobia. Freud directed Hans's father to ask questions and talk to the boy about his fears and fantasies, helping him express and understand his feelings.

Freud's approach also included progressive desensitization, exposing Hans in a controlled and safe manner to horses. Hans's father would take him for walks and they would gradually get closer to the horses, allowing the boy to face his fear in a safe and controlled environment. During these exhibits, Hans was encouraged to talk about his feelings and fears, helping to desensitize the fear response associated with horses.

By acknowledging the link between his conscious fears and unconscious conflicts, Hans was able to overcome his phobia. Freud and Hans's father worked together to help the boy understand that his fears were not really linked to horses, but rather to unconscious feelings towards his father and the Oedipus complex. By bringing these feelings to awareness and working through them, Hans experienced a significant reduction in his phobic symptoms.

Intervention Strategies

In the therapeutic context of phobias, the main goal is to unveil the unconscious conflict underlying the phobia and work to reduce its intensity and impact on the patient's life. Systematic desensitization is a valuable technique used to gradually expose the patient to the feared object or situation, allowing them to confront their fears in a progressive and controlled way. Simultaneously, the interpretation of phobic symbols seeks to bring to the patient's awareness the hidden meanings behind conscious fear, promoting deep insights and broader emotional understanding.

Systematic desensitization

Systematic desensitization involves gradual, controlled exposure of the patient to the phobic object or situation, starting with low levels of exposure and progressively increasing as the patient becomes more comfortable. This method is effective in reducing the fear response associated with the phobic stimulus. For example, a patient with a fear of heights may start by looking at pictures of high places, progressing to watching videos, and eventually visiting elevated places with therapeutic support.

During the desensitization process, it is essential for the therapist to create a safe and supportive environment where the patient feels encouraged to face their fears without judgment. The therapist may also teach relaxation and breath control techniques to help the patient manage anxiety during exposures.

Symbolic Interpretation

The symbolic interpretation of phobic fears is fundamental in psychoanalysis. By understanding the symbols underlying conscious fears, patients can gain insights into the deep emotional conflicts that cause their phobias. This process involves exploring dreams, fantasies, and free associations, helping the patient identify and work through their unconscious fears.

For example, a patient with a phobia of dogs may discover, through the analysis of dreams and associations, that the fear of dogs is linked to a childhood trauma involving an authority figure that the patient unconsciously associated with a dog. By bringing these associations into awareness, the patient can begin to work through the feelings of fear and anxiety related to the original trauma, thereby reducing the intensity of the phobia.

Case Study: Treatment of Height Phobia

Consider the case of Maria, a patient with an intense phobia of heights. Maria avoided any situation that involved height, such as riding an elevator, climbing escalators, or looking out the window of a tall building. Maria's phobia significantly limited her daily and professional life, causing her great suffering.

In the therapeutic process, the therapist used systematic desensitization and symbolic interpretation to help Maria overcome her phobia. Initially, Maria was encouraged to talk about her fears and explore any associations she might have with heights. During the sessions, Maria revealed that she had a deep-seated fear of losing control and falling, which was symbolically linked to childhood experiences of loss and insecurity.

Systematic desensitization began with Maria looking at pictures of high places and gradually progressing to watching videos of people at high heights. Over time, Maria was able to visit a high-rise building with the therapist's support, practicing relaxation and breath control techniques to manage anxiety.

Throughout her treatment, Maria also worked on understanding the symbolic meanings of her phobia. Through dream interpretation and free associations, she discovered that her fear of heights was linked to feelings of insecurity and fear of losing control, which stemmed from traumatic childhood experiences. By bringing these feelings into awareness and working through them, Maria was able to significantly reduce her phobia and improve her quality of life.

Through the case study of "Little Hans" and contemporary therapeutic strategies, not only the meticulous description of these conditions but also the practical application of therapeutic techniques for their resolution were demonstrated. By understanding the internal dynamics that generate phobias, therapists are able to help patients overcome their paralyzing fears, promoting greater psychic and emotional balance.

The detailed case analysis of "Little Hans" illustrates how psychoanalysis can reveal the hidden meanings of phobic fears and provide a path to healing. Through the combination of systematic desensitization and symbolic interpretation, patients can gain a deeper understanding of their inner conflicts and achieve lasting relief from their phobias.

In addition, the practical examples presented demonstrate the effectiveness of therapeutic strategies in addressing phobias. By creating a safe and supportive environment, and by utilizing techniques of gradual exposure and symbolic interpretation, therapists can help patients face and overcome their fears, promoting a more balanced and satisfying life.

Practical Application of Psychoanalytic Strategies

Psychoanalytic strategies for the treatment of phobias are not limited only to the cases described. They can be applied to a variety of phobias, each with its own particularities and challenges. The key to therapeutic success lies in the therapist's ability to tailor techniques to the individual needs of each patient, providing personalized and effective treatment.

Social Phobia: A Case Study

Another example is social phobia treatment, which involves an intense and persistent fear of social or performance situations in which the person may be observed and judged by others. John, a young adult with social phobia, avoided any social interaction that involved public speaking, attending meetings, or even making friends.

During therapy, the therapist used systematic desensitization and symbolic interpretation to help John cope with and overcome his social phobia. Initially, John was encouraged to talk about his experiences and fears related to social situations. He revealed that he was afraid of being ridiculed or judged negatively, which was linked to traumatic experiences of childhood bullying.

Systematic desensitization began with John practicing simple social interactions, such as greeting strangers or participating in small talk. Gradually, he progressed to more challenging situations, such as speaking in small groups and eventually giving presentations in public. The therapist taught relaxation and breath control techniques to help John manage anxiety during these exposures.

Simultaneously, the symbolic interpretation of John's fears revealed that his fear of being judged was linked to deep feelings of inadequacy and low self-esteem, stemming from his traumatic experiences. By bringing these feelings into awareness and working through them, John was able to gain insight into his insecurities and develop greater confidence in himself.

Through the analysis of the cases of "Little Hans", Mary and John, this chapter illustrated how psychoanalysis can offer a deep understanding and effective strategies for the treatment of phobias and phobic neuroses. By exploring the unconscious conflicts underlying phobic fears and utilizing systematic desensitization techniques and symbolic interpretation, therapists can help patients overcome their phobias and achieve greater psychic and emotional balance.

Psychoanalysis, with its emphasis on understanding unconscious processes, offers a unique and powerful approach to treating phobias. By recognizing the symbolic meanings of phobic fears and working to unveil the underlying emotional conflicts, therapists can assist patients in overcoming their fears and living a fuller, more fulfilling life.

Chapter 8: Defense Mechanisms and Neurosis

Defense mechanisms are the psychic guardians that protect the ego from the anxiety generated by internal conflicts. This chapter is dedicated to exploring these fundamental processes in the formation and maintenance of neuroses, delving into Freud's theories and their clinical applications through emblematic examples and detailed interpretations.

Introduction to Defense Mechanisms

Defense mechanisms, according to Freud, are unconscious strategies developed by the ego to deal with psychic content that causes anxiety. These mechanisms allow the individual to reduce distress by distorting reality or repressing thoughts, feelings, or desires that are considered unacceptable or threatening to the conscious ego. Detailed understanding of these mechanisms is essential not only for psychoanalytic theory, but also for clinical practice in the treatment of neuroses.

Main Defense Mechanisms

1. **Repression:** This mechanism operates by keeping out of consciousness content that is disturbing or threatening to the ego. For example, an individual who has been the victim of a traumatic car accident may repress specific memories of the event to avoid reliving the associated distress. Repression is considered the basis for other defense mechanisms, as it involves the withdrawal of painful impulses or desires from consciousness.
2. **Denial:** Denial is the conscious or unconscious refusal to accept a reality that causes anxiety. For example, a patient diagnosed with a terminal illness may deny their condition to avoid facing the fear of imminent death. Denial can be observed in situations of loss, where the individual refuses to accept the death of a loved one, thus prolonging the grieving process.
3. **Projection:** This mechanism involves attributing to other people or objects unacceptable feelings, desires, or impulses that are, in fact, the individual's own. For example, a patient who has unrecognized violent desires may project these feelings onto other people, seeing them as a constant threat. Projection can create a cycle of mistrust and conflict, hindering interpersonal relationships.
4. **Rationalization:** This consists of justifying behaviors, feelings, or desires in a way that seems logically and socially acceptable, even if the true underlying cause is something else. For example, a student who doesn't study for an exam may rationalize his behavior by

saying that "it's not important," when in fact he's afraid of failing. Rationalization allows the individual to avoid the guilt and shame associated with their true motivations.

5. **Displacement:** This mechanism involves redirecting impulses or emotions from a dangerous object or person to another that is less threatening. For example, an employee who is frustrated with their boss may shift their anger onto family members, treating them disproportionately. Displacement protects the individual from the consequences of confronting the real source of their anger or fear.

Role in the Formation of Neurosis

Defense mechanisms are crucial in the genesis of neuroses, because when they are used excessively or inappropriately, they can lead to the emergence of neurotic symptoms. For example, an individual who consistently suppresses sexual desires may develop symptoms of anxiety or depression as a result of the unresolved internal conflict between their unconscious desires and their conscious beliefs.

The clinical analysis of defense mechanisms in cases of neurosis offers a window into the underlying psychic conflicts. Through the interpretation of symptoms and the dynamics of the defenses used, psychoanalysts can help patients to bring repressed content to the surface, facilitating the process of resolving emotional conflicts.

Clinical Examples

1. **Case Study: "The Wolf Man"**

Freud described the case of the "Wolf Man," where the patient, Sergei Pankejeff, manifested a range of severe neurotic symptoms, including phobias and intense anxieties. The analysis revealed that these symptoms were linked to repressed memories of their childhood, especially related to sexual trauma. The repression of these painful experiences was one of the key defense mechanisms that contributed to the formation of his neurosis.

Case Breakdown

Sergei Pankejeff, nicknamed the "Wolf Man" due to a dream he had about wolves, sought help from Freud to treat his intense bouts of anxiety and depression. In the dream, Pankejeff saw several white wolves sitting in a tree, staring blankly at him. Freud interpreted this dream as a symbolic representation of the repressed sexual traumas Pankejeff had suffered in childhood.

Freud believed that wolves symbolized father figures and the tree represented the setting of a traumatic childhood scene, where Pankejeff is said to have witnessed a sexual relationship between his parents. This event, repressed because it was unacceptable to the young Sergei, manifested itself in his adult life as a neurosis. The repression of this memory and the subsequent projection of their fears and anxieties into everyday situations illustrate how defense mechanisms operate in the formation of neuroses.

Freud therapy involved bringing these repressed memories to consciousness and interpreting their symbolic meanings. Pankejeff, by recognizing the source of his symptoms, was able to begin to work with his feelings of fear and anxiety in a more conscious way, thus reducing the intensity of his neurotic symptoms.

2. Case Study: "Anna O."

Another emblematic example is the case of "Anna O." (Bertha Pappenheim), treated by Josef Breuer and documented by Freud. Anna O. suffered from a variety of symptoms, including paralysis, visual and auditory disturbances, and dissociative states. Breuer's analysis revealed that these symptoms were somatic expressions of repressed psychic conflicts.

Case Breakdown

Anna O. had a series of unexplained physical symptoms, such as partial paralysis, difficulty speaking, and episodes of temporary blindness and deafness. These symptoms began after the death of her father, with whom she had a very close relationship. Breuer's therapy involved the use of what he called a "talking cure," where Anna O. was encouraged to speak freely about her memories and associations.

Through this process, Anna O. began to reveal a number of traumatic memories and repressed emotions related to her father's death and other stressful experiences in her life. For example, she recalled caring for her father during his terminal illness, an experience that was extremely traumatic for her. The repression of these memories and the denial of feelings of pain and loss contributed to the development of her somatic symptoms.

Through "talking healing," Anna O. was able to bring these repressed memories and emotions to the surface, process them, and integrate them into her consciousness. This process led to a significant reduction in their physical symptoms, demonstrating how the expression and resolution of unconscious conflicts can alleviate neurosis.

Psychoanalytic Interpretation

The application of defense mechanisms in psychoanalytic analysis is not only limited to the identification of symptoms, but also to the understanding of how these mechanisms operate dynamically to protect the ego from threatening content. By working with the patient to explore these defensive processes, the therapist can help build a pathway to the resolution of the underlying conflicts and the relief of neurotic symptoms.

Therapeutic Process

In psychoanalytic treatment, the therapist uses various techniques to help the patient identify and understand their defense mechanisms. One such technique is dream analysis, where unconscious contents often manifest themselves in a symbolic way. By interpreting the patient's dreams, the therapist can reveal repressed desires and conflicts, helping the patient to better understand their defenses and the underlying conflicts.

Another technique is free association, where the patient is encouraged to speak freely about anything that comes to mind, without censorship. This process can bring up repressed thoughts and feelings, allowing the therapist to identify the defense mechanisms at work and help the patient work through them.

Transference is another crucial element in psychoanalytic therapy. As the patient projects unconscious feelings and attitudes toward the therapist, the therapist can use these transferential reactions to better understand the patient's conflicts and defenses. By exploring transference, the therapist can help the patient resolve unconscious conflicts and reduce reliance on dysfunctional defense mechanisms.

Practical Examples of Intervention

1. Treatment of Projection in Patients With Paranoid Personality Disorder

Patients with paranoid personality disorder often use projection as a defense mechanism, attributing to others their own feelings of hostility and distrust. An example is the case of John, who constantly believed that his co-workers were conspiring against him.

Case Breakdown

John exhibited paranoid behavior, believing that his classmates were always talking badly about him behind his back and planning to harm him. In therapy, the therapist helped John explore these feelings of distrust and hostility, revealing that they were actually rooted in past experiences of rejection and betrayal.

By working through sessions of free association and interpretation of projected feelings, John began to realize that his fears of conspiracy were actually a projection of his own insecurities and fears of rejection. This insight allowed John to work through his feelings of vulnerability and reduce the intensity of his paranoid projections.

2. Use of Rationalization in Cases of Performance Anxiety

Rationalization is often used by individuals who face performance anxiety, such as students or professionals who fear failure. Maria, a college student, often justified her poor academic performance with excuses that masked her true fear of failure.

Case Breakdown

Maria faced a paralyzing fear of failing her exams, which led her to procrastinate and avoid studying. She often rationalized her behavior by saying that exams weren't important or that she worked better under pressure. In therapy, the therapist helped Maria explore these patterns of rationalization and connect with her true fears and insecurities.

Through techniques of free association and analysis of thought patterns, Maria began to recognize that her rationalizations were a defense against the fear of not being good enough. By working through these feelings of inadequacy, Maria was able to develop healthier strategies for coping with her performance anxiety, improving both her emotional well-being and her academic performance.

By exploring clinical and theoretical examples, it was possible to elucidate how these mechanisms work to protect the ego from distress while contributing to the complexity of neurotic manifestations.

A deep understanding of defense mechanisms offers psychoanalysts a crucial tool to help patients overcome their internal conflicts and achieve a state of greater psychic balance. By identifying and working through these mechanisms, therapists can help patients reduce anxiety and neurotic symptoms, promoting greater integration and emotional health.

Through psychoanalytic analysis and intervention, patients can develop a better understanding of themselves and their internal processes, allowing them to live a more balanced and satisfying life. Psychoanalysis, with its emphasis on the exploration of unconscious processes, continues to offer a powerful and effective approach to the treatment of neuroses and other psychological disorders.

Chapter 9: Psychosexual Development and Neurosis

Sigmund Freud's theory of psychosexual development is a cornerstone in understanding neuroses. This chapter explores in detail the five phases of psychosexual development proposed by Freud, examining how fixations and regressions in these stages can influence the formation of neuroses, illustrated with clinical examples and emblematic cases.

Stages of Psychosexual Development

Freud postulated that psychosexual development occurs in discrete stages, each characterized by specific sources of pleasure and conflict. These phases are crucial for the formation of adult personality and for understanding how early experiences can impact later neurotic behavior.

1. **Oral Phase**: This phase encompasses the early period of life, where the mouth is the main source of pleasure and exploration. Nutrition through breastfeeding or bottle feeding is critical for psychosexual development. Freud discussed at length how eating experiences can lead to oral fixations, subsequently influencing neurotic behaviors such as the pursuit of oral pleasures in unhealthy ways such as smoking, compulsive eating, or addictive behaviors.

   Clinical Example: Freud analyzed the case of "Dora," a young woman whose hostility toward her father was interpreted as an unresolved oral fixation, manifested by neurotic symptoms such as chronic cough and irritability.

2. **Anal Phase**: During this phase, the focus of pleasure shifts to activities related to the control and elimination of bodily waste. Acquisition and retention of sphincter control are essential. Freud noted that conflicts at this stage can result in anal-retentive (rigidity, excessive order) or anal-expulsive (disorganization, impulsivity) fixations.

   Clinical Example: The case of "The Wolf Man" exemplifies how excessive retention or uncontrollable release during the anal phase can reflect unresolved conflicts and contribute to the formation of neurotic symptoms such as obsessions and compulsions.

3. **Phallic Phase**: This phase is marked by the development of the genital erogenous zone and curiosity about the differences between the sexes. The Oedipus and Electra Complex emerges at this stage, where the child develops loving desires for the parent of the opposite sex and hostility for the parent of the

same sex. Unresolved conflicts at this stage can lead to fixations that influence gender identity and patterns of sexual behavior in adulthood.

Clinical Example: Freud explored the case of "Dora," where the patient's refusal to accept Mr. K's sexual advances reflected an unresolved phallic conflict with her father, contributing to later neurotic symptoms such as hysteria and anxiety.

4. **Latency Phase**: During this phase, sexual drives are suppressed and psychic energy is directed toward educational and social activities. Freud argued that latency offers a pause in active sexual development, but unresolved conflicts in earlier phases can resurface in this phase, especially in response to external stressors.

Clinical Example: In "The Case of Little Hans," Freud interpreted the boy's phobia of horses as a symbolic return to unresolved phallic conflicts, where horses represented the father and fears were a way of dealing with feelings of castration.

5. **Genital Phase**: This phase marks sexual maturation, where romantic and sexual interest is directed outside the family to peers. Healthy development through the earlier stages facilitates the formation of intimate relationships and proper sexual fulfillment.

Clinical Example: In "The Rat Man," Freud investigated how the patient's early oral and anal fixation negatively impacted their social and emotional abilities in adulthood, contributing to neurotic symptoms such as obsessive-compulsive neurosis.

Fixations and Regressions

Fixations occur when psychosexual development is halted at a specific stage, while regressions are temporary returns to earlier stages in response to stress. Both phenomena can contribute significantly to the formation of neuroses, influencing the adult personality and the way in which psychic conflicts are manifested.

Clinical Example: "Anna O." presented hysterical symptoms, such as paralysis and hallucinations, which Freud interpreted as a regression to the oral phase, where unresolved conflicts around eating and emotional dependence led to the conversion of these conflicts into physical symptoms.

Impact on the Formation of Neuroses

Freud's theory of psychosexual development provides an essential framework for understanding how childhood experiences shape the adult psyche. Fixations on specific phases can predispose individuals to distinct neurotic traits, such as obsessions, phobias, or compulsive behaviors. Psychoanalytic therapy aims to tap into these fixations, bringing to awareness the underlying unconscious conflicts and promoting healthy psychosexual development.

By examining psychosexual development through the lens of psychoanalysis, we are able to discern how early experiences shape neurotic features and symptoms manifest in adulthood. Understanding the stages of psychosexual development not only enriches our therapeutic approach, but also sheds light on the deep origins of neuroses and how we can intervene effectively to promote psychological well-being.

Chapter 10: Transference and Countertransference

Transference and countertransference represent essential pillars of psychoanalytic practice, unraveling the complexities of interpersonal relationships within the therapeutic setting. This chapter explores in depth these fundamental concepts, their importance in understanding neuroses, and their practical application in psychoanalytic therapy.

Concepts and Importance in Therapy

In his theoretical development, Sigmund Freud introduced the concept of transference as a phenomenon in which patients project unconscious feelings, desires, and fantasies onto the therapist. This process is crucial as it allows the patient to relive past meaningful relationships in a safe and controlled context. By projecting unresolved emotions onto the therapist, the patient offers the analyst a privileged window into the inner conflicts that permeate his or her psyche.

Countertransference, on the other hand, refers to the therapist's emotional response to the patient's projections. Initially seen by Freud as an interference with analysis, countertransference has evolved to be recognized as a valuable source of information about the patient's unconscious processes. In this way, countertransference can be understood not only as a noise in the analysis, but as a channel for deep insights into the patient's emotional dynamics.

"Dora" Case: Transference and Countertransference in Action

To illustrate, let us consider the classic case of "Dora", analyzed by Freud. Dora, whose real name was Ida Bauer, had complex neurotic symptoms, including asthma attacks, which were interpreted as manifestations of unconscious conflicts related to sexual desires and repressed feelings toward her father and Mr. K. Through transference, Dora projected these conflicts onto Freud himself, offering crucial insights that shaped his analysis and interpretation.

During treatment, Freud noticed that Dora transferred to him ambivalent feelings that originally belonged to his relationships with his father and Mr. K. She showed a mixture of affection and anger, reflecting his unresolved inner conflicts. Freud, on the other hand, experienced strong emotional responses, indicating the presence of countertransference. He acknowledged that his own irritation and frustration, in part, reflected his personal experiences and the unique dynamic created with Dora.

Dynamics of Transference in Neurosis

In neurosis, transference plays a vital role in revealing the repressed contents and emotional conflicts that perpetuate neurotic symptoms. For example, a patient with obsessive-compulsive neurosis may manifest a transference where they idealize the therapist as an authoritarian or paternal figure, reflecting unresolved conflicts related to authority and unconscious guilt.

Let's explore a fictitious example, based on psychoanalytic principles. Imagine a patient named John who has an obsessive-compulsive neurosis. John often sees his therapist as an authoritarian and infallible figure, transferring to him the feelings of wonder and fear that originally belonged to his father. During sessions, John may express an intense need to please the therapist and rigidly follow their suggestions, while at the same time feeling anxious and guilty about any minor perceived flaws.

By exploring these transference dynamics, the therapist can help John recognize that his overreactions and obsessive behavior are linked to his childhood history with his father. This insight can allow John to work through his feelings of guilt and anxiety, developing a more balanced relationship with both the therapist figure and other authority figures in his life.

Countertransference Management

Countertransference, while a valuable tool, requires sophisticated clinical skills to be properly managed. The therapist must be aware of his or her own emotional responses, recognizing when these may be influenced by the therapist's own internal conflicts or personal history.

Let's consider a fictional therapist, Dr. Maria, who is treating a patient named Peter, who is showing symptoms of hysteria. During the sessions, Dr. Maria notices that she feels irritated and impatient with Pedro's tendency to dramatize her problems. As she reflects on these emotions, Dr. Maria recognizes that her irritation may be related to her own past experiences where intense emotional expressions were discouraged in her family.

Aware of this dynamic, Dr. Maria uses her countertransference reactions to better understand Pedro's emotional world. She realizes that Peter's role-playing may be a way of seeking attention and validation that he never properly received. By discussing her observations with Pedro, Dr. Maria helps him explore these needs and find healthier ways to express his emotions and seek support.

Detailed Examples of Overcoming in Therapy
John's Case: Obsessive-Compulsive Transference

John, throughout therapy, was encouraged to talk freely about his memories and feelings towards authority figures, especially his father. Initially, John had difficulty connecting his current anxieties with his past experiences. However, through techniques of free association and dream interpretation, he began to realize how his compulsive behavior was a way of coping with guilt and the need for paternal approval.

For example, John recalled a recurring dream where he was constantly cleaning his house, but he could never get it perfectly clean. Freud interpreted this dream as a metaphor for John's relentless pursuit of approval and inability to feel good enough. As John discussed this interpretation, he began to understand that his obsession with cleanliness was a way of trying to gain the approval he felt he had lost in childhood.

Throughout the sessions, the therapist helped John reassess his expectations and develop a more realistic self-image. John began to accept that he didn't have to be perfect to be accepted and loved. This recognition led to a significant decrease in his obsessive behaviors, allowing him to live a more balanced life that was less controlled by anxiety.

Maria's Case: Transference and Relationship Conflicts

Maria, a fictional patient, sought therapy due to recurring problems in her romantic relationships. She often chose emotionally unavailable partners, which resulted in feelings of rejection and low self-esteem. During therapy, it became evident that Maria transferred unresolved feelings related to her father, who was distant and critical, to her partners.

Maria's therapist, observing her intense emotional reactions during discussions about her relationships, used countertransference to gain insights into Maria's emotional dynamics. The therapist noted that she felt protective and sometimes frustrated by Maria's tendency to repeat self-destructive patterns. As she reflected on these emotions, the therapist realized that Maria was recreating the dynamic of rejection and approval-seeking that she experienced with her father.

Working with these insights, the therapist helped Maria explore her expectations and beliefs about love and intimacy. Maria began to recognize that she was looking to her partners for the validation she never received from her father. With this understanding, Maria was able to work through her pain and develop a healthier view of herself and her emotional needs.

At the end of therapy, Maria reported feeling more confident and able to choose partners who offered emotional support and reciprocity. This progress represented a significant change, where Maria was able to break the cycle of dysfunctional relationships and find greater satisfaction and balance in her love life.

Integration of Transfer and Countertransference in Therapy

An understanding of transference and countertransference is essential to the clinical practice of psychoanalysis, especially in the treatment of neuroses. These concepts not only enrich the understanding of the psychic mechanisms at play, but also provide a path for resolving the internal conflicts that feed neurotic symptoms. By integrating transference and countertransference in a reflective and analytical manner, psychoanalytic therapists can offer a profoundly enriching and transformative therapeutic intervention to their patients.

Hansel and Gretel's detailed examples demonstrate how careful analysis of transference and countertransference can lead to powerful insights and the resolution of dysfunctional emotional patterns. By exploring the unconscious dynamics that emerge in the therapeutic relationship, both patients and therapists can work together to achieve greater self-knowledge and emotional growth.

Freud laid the foundation for these practices, and contemporary psychoanalysis continues to evolve, integrating new understandings and techniques to enhance the effectiveness of treatment. Transference and countertransference remain central to exploring the complex earthly depths of the human mind, offering a pathway to healing and profound transformation.

Chapter 11: Freud's Classical Case Analysis

In this chapter, we will take a deep dive into some of the most emblematic classical cases treated by Sigmund Freud, highlighting their complexities, the psychoanalytic techniques applied, and the interpretations that shed light on the underlying neurotic mechanisms. Each case offers a unique window into understanding the neuroses and therapeutic strategies developed by Freud.

Famous Cases Review

Freud, throughout his career, documented several case studies that became cornerstones of psychoanalysis. Two such cases, "The Wolf Man" and "Dora," vividly exemplify how unconscious conflicts can manifest in complex neurotic symptoms and how psychoanalysis seeks to unravel these mysteries of the mind.

"The Wolf Man": A Case Study of Child Hysteria

We revisit here the case of the "Wolf Man", about the young Sergei Pankejeff, who developed a series of severe neurotic symptoms after a traumatic incident involving wolves. Freud diagnosed him with infantile hysteria, characterized by symptoms such as recurring nightmares, intense fears, and complex phobias. Detailed study of this case revealed that the patient's symptoms were symbolic manifestations of unresolved Oedipal conflicts and unconscious fantasies. Psychoanalytic interpretation revealed that wolves symbolized ambivalent father figures and hysterical symptoms served as defenses against unacceptable desires.

Case Breakdown

Sergei Pankejeff, whom Freud nicknamed the "Wolf Man" due to a remarkable dream he had as a child, had severe symptoms of anxiety and depression. In the dream, Pankejeff saw several white wolves sitting in a tree, staring blankly at him. Freud interpreted this dream as a symbolic representation of repressed sexual traumas that Pankejeff had suffered in childhood.

Therapeutic Process

Freud used the technique of free association to explore Pankejeff's associations with the dream of wolves. During the sessions, Pankejeff talked about his childhood memories and the relationships with his parents. Freud believed that wolves symbolized father figures and that the tree represented the setting of a traumatic childhood scene, where Pankejeff is said to have witnessed a sexual relationship between his parents. This event, repressed because it was unacceptable to the young Sergei, manifested itself in his adult life as a neurosis.

By bringing up these repressed memories and interpreting their symbolic meanings, Pankejeff began to recognize the source of his symptoms. Freud helped Pankejeff work through his feelings of fear and anxiety in a more conscious way, thus reducing the intensity of his neurotic symptoms.

Overcoming in Therapy

During therapy, Pankejeff went through several phases of resistance and insight. Initially, there was strong resistance to accepting Freud's interpretation of the traumatic events of his childhood. However, as therapy progressed, Pankejeff began to accept the connection between his symptoms and the repressed events. Through continuous sessions, he was able to express his repressed emotions, such as anger and fear, and to integrate these experiences into his consciousness.

The therapy resulted in a significant reduction in Pankejeff's symptoms, allowing him to lead a more functional life that was less plagued by irrational anxieties. This case demonstrated the efficacy of psychoanalysis in treating complex neuroses through the exploration and resolution of unconscious conflicts.

"Dora": A Case of Hysteria and Sexual Conflict

Again to the "Dora" case, where a young woman, Ida Bauer, presented symptoms such as unexplained cough, loss of voice and depression. Freud identified Dora's symptoms as manifestations of an unresolved sexual conflict involving her father and the family friend. The analysis revealed that coughing and loss of voice functioned as symbolic substitutes for expressing their anger and repressed desire. Dream interpretation and free association were crucial techniques used by Freud to bring out these unconscious contents, allowing the patient to deal with her internal conflicts in a more conscious and integrative way.

Case Breakdown

Ida Bauer, known in this case as "Dora," was brought to Freud at the age of 18, suffering from a range of hysterical symptoms, including a persistent nervous cough, aphonia (loss of voice) and bouts of depression. Freud soon realized that these symptoms were related to a love triangle involving his father, the wife of a family friend (Frau K.), and the family friend himself (Herr K.).

Therapeutic Process

Freud used dream interpretation and the technique of free association to unravel Dora's unconscious conflicts. One particularly significant dream involved Dora walking in an unfamiliar city, looking for a specific location but never finding it. Freud interpreted this dream as a representation of Dora's search for love and acceptance, something she was unable to achieve due to the complex family and sexual dynamics around her.

During therapy, Dora revealed episodes of inappropriate sexual advances by Herr K., which her father ignored or minimized, possibly due to his own involvement with Frau K. This internal conflict between his desire for recognition and protection from his father, and the perceived betrayal, manifested itself in Dora's physical symptoms.

Overcoming in Therapy

Through analysis, Dora began to understand that her coughing and loss of voice were unconscious ways of expressing her anger and frustration with her father and Herr K. By acknowledging and verbalizing these repressed feelings, she was able to begin to work through them in a conscious way. Freud also helped Dora realize that her resistance to treatment was linked to her ambivalence toward the men in her life and the fear of facing these conflicts directly.

Although Dora stopped therapy abruptly, the insights she gained during her sessions with Freud were significant. Not only did they help alleviate some of his symptoms, but they also provided a deeper understanding of his inner conflicts. This case highlighted the importance of addressing both the manifest symptoms and the underlying conflicts in psychoanalytic therapy.

Psychoanalytic Interpretation and Conclusions

Each classic case analyzed by Freud not only illustrates the complex dynamics of neuroses, but also validates the psychoanalytic theories developed by him. Repression, defense mechanisms, transference and countertransference emerge as fundamental elements in the formation and treatment of neuroses. Through meticulous analysis of the cases of "The Wolf Man" and "Dora," Freud set a precedent for psychoanalytic clinical practice, demonstrating how the unresolved conflicts of the past can echo in profound ways in patients' presents.

Role of Transference and Countertransference

Transference, where patients project unconscious feelings and attitudes onto the therapist, and countertransference, where the therapist reacts with their own unconscious feelings, play crucial roles in psychoanalytic therapy. In both cases, Freud used transference to better understand patients' internal conflicts. For example, in Dora's case, her transference of anger and frustration to Freud reflected her unresolved feelings toward her father, and Herr K. Freud used these transference reactions to help Dora confront and understand her unconscious conflicts.

Conclusions on Defence Mechanisms

Defense mechanisms, such as the repression observed in Pankejeff and the displacement and projection in Dora, were fundamental to the formation of her neurotic symptoms. Psychoanalytic analysis has shown that by bringing to awareness these mechanisms and the conflicts they mask, it is possible to alleviate symptoms and promote a healthier psychic integration.

The repression of Pankejeff's sexual traumas and Oedipal desires led to the manifestation of hysterical and phobic symptoms, while Dora's defense mechanisms were linked to her inability to directly express her anger and desire. The therapy allowed both patients to recognize and work through these conflicts, highlighting the effectiveness of psychoanalysis in treating complex neuroses.

Contemporary Impact

The conclusions drawn from these cases continue to inform contemporary psychoanalysis, highlighting the importance of a holistic and interpretive approach to understanding and treating the complexities of the human mind. A deep understanding of defense, transference, and countertransference mechanisms provides psychoanalysts with essential tools to help patients overcome their internal conflicts and achieve a state of greater psychic balance.

Freud's classic cases not only validate his theories but also provide a solid foundation for modern clinical practice. They exemplify how exploring unconscious conflicts and defense mechanisms can lead to deep insights and resolution of neurotic symptoms. Freud's detailed and thoughtful approach remains a cornerstone in psychoanalytic treatment, demonstrating the importance of understanding the past in order to heal the present.

Chapter 12: Modern Approaches to the Therapy of Neuroses

Psychoanalysis, since its conception by Sigmund Freud, has evolved significantly, integrating new theories, techniques, and perspectives that broaden our understanding and therapeutic approach to neuroses. This chapter explores theoretical and practical updates in contemporary psychoanalysis, highlighting how these developments enrich the treatment of neurotic conditions. In addition, the integration of other complementary therapeutic approaches is discussed, aiming to provide a more complete and effective intervention for patients.

Theoretical and Practical Updates

Since Freud, several theorists and psychoanalysts have contributed to expanding and revising the foundations of psychoanalysis. Jacques Lacan, for example, brought a new perspective by emphasizing the importance of language and symbolic structure in the formation of neurotic symptoms. For Lacan, symptoms are manifestations of structural conflicts between the subject and language, adding a layer of complexity to the understanding of neuroses.

Ana's Case: Language and Symbolic Structure

Ana, a fictitious patient, had symptoms of intense anxiety and communication difficulties. Lacanian analysis revealed that her symptoms were deeply rooted in how she internalized language. Anne often felt unable to express her needs and emotions due to a rigid symbolic structure in her psyche. During therapy, as she worked with the signifiers of her personal and family language, Ana began to understand how her words and the linguistic structure she adopted influenced her feelings and behaviors.

By identifying and reinterpreting these signifiers, Ana began to experience a significant reduction in her anxiety and an improvement in her communicative skills. This Lacanian approach not only elucidated the root of her symptoms, but also offered a path to transformation by allowing Anne to reconstruct her relationship with language and communication.

Melanie Klein, on the other hand, focused on the importance of object relations and the early mother-infant dynamics in the formation of psychic conflicts. His contributions emphasized the importance of identifications and unconscious fantasies in determining neurotic symptoms, especially in children and adolescents.

Luke's Case: Object Relations and Unconscious Fantasies

Lucas, a fictional teenager, struggled with intense feelings of inadequacy and anger, often directed against authority figures. The Kleinian approach focused on his unconscious fantasies and the primary relationship with his mother. During therapy, it became clear that Lucas had internalized a highly critical and punitive maternal image, which he projected onto his teachers and other authority figures.

As he worked through the sessions, Lucas was encouraged to explore these identifications and express his unconscious fantasies. This process allowed him to identify and revise the internal images that influenced his feelings of inadequacy and anger. As a result, Lucas began to develop a more balanced relationship with authority, feeling less threatened and more competent in his interactions.

Donald Winnicott, through the concept of the transitional object, explored how the processes of transition between internal and external reality impact emotional development and the formation of neurotic symptoms. Winnicott brought a more relational and environment-focused approach to enabling psychic growth, profoundly influencing contemporary clinical practices.

Sofia's Case: Transitional Objects and Enabling Environment

Sofia, a fictional young adult, had an intense dependence on specific objects, such as a childhood blanket, to feel safe. The Winnicottian approach focused on understanding these transitional objects and the role they played in their emotional life. During therapy, Sofia was encouraged to reflect on the meaning of these objects and how they served as a point of connection between her inner and outer reality.

As she explored these connections, Sofia began to realize that her dependence on these objects was related to an unstable family environment during her childhood. Therapy created a safe space where Sofia was able to develop new ways to feel safe and connected, gradually reducing her dependence on transitional objects and increasing her ability to face the challenges of adulthood with greater resilience.

Integration of Other Therapeutic Approaches

Although psychoanalysis remains the theoretical and clinical basis for the treatment of neuroses, the integration of other therapeutic approaches has significantly enriched the field of psychotherapy. Cognitive Behavioral Therapy (CBT), for example, offers structured, goal-oriented techniques focusing on modifying dysfunctional thoughts and maladaptive behaviors. The combination of CBT with psychoanalysis allows for an integrative approach that not only explores the unconscious roots of neurotic symptoms, but also promotes practical strategies for dealing with these symptoms in the patient's daily life.

Marcos Case: Integration of CBT and Psychoanalysis

Mark, a fictional patient with generalized anxiety disorder, benefited from the integration of CBT with psychoanalysis. While psychoanalytic analysis explored the unconscious roots of her anxiety, revealing unresolved internal conflicts related to her childhood, CBT provided practical tools for coping with daily symptoms.

Marcos learned to identify and restructure his negative automatic thoughts through cognitive techniques, while the psychoanalytic sessions deepened his understanding of his underlying fears. This two-pronged approach allowed Marcos to not only better understand his anxieties but also develop effective strategies for managing them in everyday life.

Systemic Family Therapy, on the other hand, focuses on family dynamics and interaction patterns that contribute to the maintenance of neurotic symptoms. Integrating this approach with psychoanalysis allows for a more comprehensive understanding of the contextual factors that influence the development and manifestation of neuroses, as well as offering therapeutic support for the family system as a whole.

Clara's Case: Integration of Systemic Family Therapy and Psychoanalysis

Clara, a fictional adolescent with depressive symptoms, proved resistant to individual therapeutic approaches. The integration of systemic family therapy proved to be essential for its progress. During the family sessions, it became evident that the dynamics of dysfunctional control and communication in her family contributed significantly to her symptoms.

By combining psychoanalysis with systemic family therapy, the therapy helped Clara and her family identify unhealthy interaction patterns and develop healthier forms of communication and emotional support. Clara began to feel more understood and valued within her family, which led to a noticeable improvement in her depressive symptoms.

Epilogue

The Future of Psychoanalysis in the Treatment of Neuroses

As psychoanalysis continues to evolve, adapting to cultural and scientific changes, its role in the treatment of neuroses also transforms. Interdisciplinarity is becoming increasingly crucial, with collaborations between psychoanalysts, neuroscientists, cognitive psychologists and other mental health professionals. These collaborations not only enrich the theoretical basis of psychoanalysis, but also promote the development of new therapeutic methodologies that integrate contemporary findings with the fundamental principles of Freudian psychoanalysis.

The future of psychoanalytic therapy of neuroses promises a more flexible, adaptive, and holistic approach, capable of responding to the individual needs of patients in an ever-changing world. By continuing to explore and integrate new therapeutic approaches, psychoanalysis reaffirms its relevance and effectiveness in understanding and treating the psychic complexities that characterize neuroses.

By examining how psychoanalysis has evolved from Freud to the present day, and how the contributions of contemporary theorists have expanded our understanding of neuroses, we can envision a promising future for psychoanalysis as a dynamic and effective therapeutic approach.

In this context, the combination of a solid grounding in psychoanalytic theory with the flexibility to integrate new perspectives and therapeutic techniques offers not only a more complete treatment for neurotic symptoms, but also a deeper understanding of the psychic processes that shape human experience. Thus, psychoanalysis continues to be a powerful tool to help individuals face and overcome the challenges of their neuroses, promoting lasting psychological and emotional growth.

By integrating CBT, systemic family therapy, and other modern approaches, contemporary psychoanalysis offers a richer, more multifaceted therapeutic intervention. This evolution allows therapists to approach neuroses with a theoretical depth and practical effectiveness that reflects the complexities and diversities of the human mind.

The journey through psychoanalysis and neurosis is, in many ways, an exploration of the mysteries of the human mind. Sigmund Freud, with his intellectual boldness and his dedication to understanding the unconscious, blazed trails that transformed psychology and psychotherapy. This book, in revisiting his contributions and the cases he studied, reminds us of the importance of continuing this exploration.

The study of neuroses, as we have seen, reveals the depth of the emotional conflicts that can arise within us. Each type of neurosis, be it hysteria, obsessive-compulsive neurosis, phobia, or anxiety, shows us different ways in which the human mind deals with suffering and repressed desires. The classic cases we analyzed, such as those of Anna O., Dora, and the Rat Man, offer windows into these internal dynamics, illuminating the paths that psychoanalysis can follow to promote healing.

Psychoanalysis, with its focus on exploring the unconscious, offers a therapeutic approach that is both profound and transformative. Through free association, dream interpretation, and resistance analysis, psychoanalysts can help patients unravel the hidden meanings of their symptoms and resolve underlying emotional conflicts. This approach not only alleviates suffering but also promotes greater self-awareness and personal growth.

Freud's legacy is undoubtedly immense. His theories about the unconscious, defense mechanisms, and the dynamics of repressed desires continue to profoundly influence psychology and psychotherapy. However, psychoanalysis is not static; It evolves and adapts, incorporating new ideas and methods. The contemporary practice of psychoanalysis, while based on the fundamental principles established by Freud, also benefits from the contributions of subsequent generations of psychoanalysts and the discoveries of neuroscience and modern psychology.

The study of neuroses is ultimately an exploration of the human condition. Neurotic symptoms, with all their variety and complexity, are expressions of the internal struggles we all face at some point in our lives. Psychoanalysis offers us a way to understand these struggles and to find paths to healing. By bringing repressed conflicts and desires to light, psychoanalysis helps us integrate these experiences in a healthy and productive way, promoting deeper emotional well-being.

This book, by revisiting Freud's contributions and the cases he studied, offers a rich and detailed view of neuroses and psychoanalysis. We hope that by the end of this reading, you will have not only a deeper understanding of neuroses, but also a broader appreciation of psychoanalysis and its vital role in understanding and treating psychological disorders.

The human mind is a vast and mysterious field, and psychoanalysis continues to be a powerful tool for exploring this field. By understanding the mechanisms of the unconscious and the emotional conflicts that shape our behavior, we can not only alleviate suffering but also promote deeper personal growth and self-knowledge.

The journey through psychoanalysis and neurosis does not end here. Each new case, each new discovery, offers us new opportunities to learn and grow. Psychoanalysis, with its detailed and empathetic approach, continues to be an inexhaustible source of insight and inspiration for all who seek to understand the human mind.

May this book be an invitation to continue that journey, exploring the mysteries of the unconscious and unlocking the secrets of neurosis. By delving into the depths of the human mind, we can discover not only the repressed conflicts and desires, but also the extraordinary capacity for healing and transformation that resides within each of us.

The exploration of neuroses through psychoanalysis reveals to us not only the depth and complexity of the human mind, but also the remarkable ability of psychoanalysis to provide insights and avenues for healing. This book, which thoroughly analyzed different forms of neurosis, illustrated how the psychoanalytic principles and methods developed by Sigmund Freud continue to be vital to the understanding and treatment of these psychological disorders.

From the classic case studies, such as those of Anna O., Dora and the Rat Man, we have been able to see how Freud and his followers used free association, dream interpretation and resistance analysis to unravel the unconscious conflicts that underpinned neurotic symptoms. These cases not only illustrated the therapeutic processes but also highlighted the importance of addressing emotional distress in a way that allows patients to integrate and resolve their internal conflicts.

Psychoanalysis, in dealing with neurosis, reveals that symptoms are not merely problems to be eliminated, but manifestations of deep emotional conflicts that need to be understood and resolved. Freud showed that by bringing these conflicts to consciousness, through careful and empathetic analysis, it is possible to alleviate the symptoms and promote greater psychic integration. This approach offers a valuable perspective not only for the treatment of neuroses, but also for a broader understanding of the human condition.

The chapters in this book have detailed the specific characteristics and dynamics of different types of neurosis, from hysteria to obsessive-compulsive neurosis. Each form of neurosis presents its own complexities and challenges, but they all share the common characteristic of being expressions of unconscious conflicts. Through the analysis of these cases, we were able to see how psychoanalysis can offer a deep understanding and an effective therapeutic approach to these conditions.

Hysteria, with its varied somatic and emotional manifestations, exemplifies how physical symptoms can be a conversion of emotional conflicts. Case studies like Anna O.'s show how exploring underlying emotional traumas can lead to symptom resolution. Similarly, the analysis of obsessive-compulsive neurosis, through the case of the Rat Man, illustrates how compulsive rituals are attempts to control the anxiety generated by oedipal conflicts and repressed desires. Through the analysis of these conflicts, it is possible to alleviate obsessive-compulsive symptoms and promote a greater understanding of oneself.

The insights gained through psychoanalysis are not just theoretical; They have significant practical implications for therapy. Understanding defense mechanisms, such as repression and projection, and the ability to interpret symbols in patients' dreams and free associations, are valuable tools for therapists. These methods allow for a therapeutic approach that goes beyond the simple suppression of symptoms, aiming at a deeper and more lasting resolution of emotional conflicts.

The relevance of psychoanalysis for the treatment of neuroses has not diminished over time. Despite the emergence of new therapeutic approaches and advances in neuroscience, the fundamental principles of psychoanalysis continue to offer valuable insights into the human mind. The ability to explore the unconscious, to understand repressed desires and fears, and to work through emotional conflicts, remains central to effective psychotherapeutic practice.

In addition, psychoanalysis offers a unique perspective on the nature of human suffering. Rather than seeing neurotic symptoms as mere dysfunctions, psychoanalysis regards them as symbolic expressions of deep inner conflicts. This view allows for a therapeutic approach that not only alleviates suffering but also promotes greater self-knowledge and personal growth.

Part 3 - Consciousness

Prologue
Are we all conscious?

1. Consciousness in Freudian Psychoanalysis: Freud's Two Topics

Maybe stupidity is just a lack of self-awareness. Of our reality, traumas, limitations, fears and desires.
Sigmund Freud's psychoanalysis was a milestone in the

understanding of consciousness, revealing that the human mind is not a simple and transparent system, but a complex field with layers and internal conflicts. Freud developed two major models, or topics, of the mind: the first, centered on the notions of **the unconscious, preconscious,** and **conscious**, and the second, which introduces the instances of the **id, ego,** and **superego**. Both models are fundamental to understand the concept of consciousness from a Freudian perspective.

1.1 First Topic: The Conscious, Preconscious, and Unconscious System

Freud elaborated his first theory of mind in 1900, with the publication of *The Interpretation of Dreams*. Here, he proposed the existence of three levels or systems that make up the human psyche: the **conscious**, the **preconscious,** and the **unconscious**. Consciousness, in this model, is not something homogeneous and accessible, but deeply segmented.

Conscious

The **conscious** system refers to the thoughts, perceptions, and sensations of which we have direct knowledge at any given time. Everything that is in our immediate attention is part of consciousness. However, Freud believed that consciousness represents only a small fraction of human mental activity, a "tip of the iceberg" of a much vaster psyche.

Preconscious

The **preconscious** is composed of mental information and content that is not immediately present in consciousness, but can be easily accessed, such as stored memories and knowledge that are not in the focus of attention. If we need to remember something, such as a person's name or what we ate yesterday, we turn to the preconscious. It is an intermediate area between the conscious and the unconscious.

Unconscious

The **unconscious** is the heart of Freudian psychoanalysis. According to Freud, this is the place where desires, impulses, repressed memories, and unresolved conflicts reside, inaccessible to consciousness in a direct way. Many of these unconscious forces are unacceptable or uncomfortable, which is why they are repressed, but they still significantly influence behavior and conscious mental life. Freud highlighted the importance of the unconscious in the formation of neurotic symptoms and in the conduct of psychic life in general.

Through processes such as dreams, faulty acts, and neurotic symptoms, the unconscious manifests itself in symbolic ways, always trying to return to consciousness, but often masked by defense mechanisms such as **repression**. Freud maintained that analytic work involved bringing these repressed contents to light, promoting a "catharsis" or emotional release.

1.2 Second Topic: Id, Ego and Superego

In 1923, Freud advanced his theory by introducing the **second topic,** a new structural model of the mind divided into three main components: the **id,** the **ego,** and the **superego.** This model is designed to explain internal psychic conflicts and the dynamics between conscious and unconscious forces.

Id

The **id** is the most primitive and instinctive part of the psyche, present from birth. It operates according to the **pleasure principle**, seeking the immediate satisfaction of biological impulses and unconscious desires. The id is entirely unconscious and irrational, governed by sexual and aggressive impulses (what Freud called the **life drive** and **the death drive**). The id does not take into account reality or social norms, being impulsive and chaotic in its pursuit of gratification.

Ego

The **ego** arises from the individual's need to deal with external reality and moderate the impulses of the id. Governed by the **reality principle**, the ego is responsible for balancing the desires of the id with the demands of the real world and social expectations. Although part of the ego is conscious, it also contains unconscious elements, since the mediation of primary impulses and external realities often involves psychic defenses. The ego acts as an "arbiter" that tries to satisfy the desires of the id in socially acceptable ways.

Superego

The **superego** represents the internalized moral norms, values, and ideals acquired through education and parental figures. It functions as the "moral conscience" of the individual, imposing ethical and cultural standards. The superego is divided into two parts: the **ego ideal**, which represents what a person aspires to be, and the **moral conscience**, which punishes the individual through guilt and shame when their actions are not in accordance with internalized values. Thus, the superego can conflict with the id, resulting in internal tensions between desire and morality.

1.3 The Conflict Between Consciousness and Unconscious

In Freudian theory, consciousness is often involved in a conflict with unconscious forces. The ego tries to navigate between the impulsive demands of the id, the moral constraints of the superego, and the realities of the external world. When the ego fails to mediate these forces efficiently, the result can be the formation of neurotic symptoms, such as anxiety or depression. The unconscious is dynamic, always active, and the repressed energies contained in it constantly seek to express themselves, even if in indirect ways.

2. The Mirror Stage in Lacan and the Formation of the Consciousness of the Self

Jacques Lacan, a French psychoanalyst, expanded Freud's theory in a significant way, especially by integrating linguistic and structural aspects to the understanding of the mind. One of the central concepts in his work is the **Mirror Stage**, which explores the development of the **self** and consciousness from a symbolic and imagery perspective. This concept offers a critical explanation of how **identity** and self-awareness arise in childhood.

2.1 The Mirror Stage: A New Understanding of the Self

Lacan introduced the idea of the **Mirror Stage** in 1936, arguing that between 6 and 18 months of age, the child experiences a crucial moment in the development of his consciousness and identity. During this stage, the child looks at himself in the mirror and, for the first time, recognizes his reflected image. This visual recognition causes a duality: on the one hand, the child identifies with the image in the mirror, but on the other hand, he realizes that his body unit is not as cohesive as the image suggests.

This experience results in the formation of the **self (moi),** an "idealized self" that arises from identification with the unified image in the mirror. For Lacan, the self that the child sees in the mirror is an "ideal", something that seems stable and complete, in contrast to the child's internal experience, which is still chaotic and fragmented. Thus, the Mirror Stage marks the beginning of **narcissism** and **alienation**, as the child begins to perceive his self through an external and idealized image, rather than through a direct and internal experience of himself.

2.2 The Division between the Real and the Symbolic

For Lacan, the consciousness of the self formed in the Mirror Stage is always linked to the **symbolic** — the world of language, signs, and representations. From the moment the child identifies with the image in the mirror, he enters what Lacan calls **the symbolic order,** where his identity and consciousness are mediated by words, symbols, and external representations. In this sense, the "I" is always something alienated, a construction that depends on language and image.

This Lacanian conception deviates from the Freudian notion of a centered and integrated ego. For Lacan, the consciousness of the self is always fragmented and divided, a result of the mediation between the **real** — which is ineffable and impossible to fully symbolize — and the symbolic. The self is, therefore, an imaginary construction, continually reformulated through language and social interactions.

3. The Johari Window and the Expansion of Interpersonal Awareness

After exploring the view of consciousness in psychoanalysis and Lacan's theory, we arrived at the **Johari Window**, an analysis tool created by psychologists **Joseph Luft** and **Harry Ingham** in 1955. Although not directly related to psychoanalysis, the Johari Window is a powerful metaphor for understanding **interpersonal consciousness** and the way the "self" is revealed and hidden in social interactions. It offers valuable insights into the dynamics between the **conscious** and the **unconscious** in the relational context.

3.1 The Johari Window Model

The Johari Window and the Expansion of Interpersonal Awareness (continued)

The **Johari Window** is a tool created to assist in understanding the self and interpersonal interactions. The model uses a four-quadrant matrix to illustrate the different aspects of the self in relation to consciousness and unknowing. Each quadrant represents a kind of relationship between what is known or unknown to ourselves and to others. Through this tool, it is possible to identify areas that can be explored and developed for greater self-awareness and to improve interpersonal relationships.

3.1 The Johari Window Model

The Johari Window divides the self into four quadrants, each representing a field of perception in relation to the knowledge of oneself and others. These quadrants are:

1. **Open Area (Arena): Known to me and others**
2. **Blind Area: Unknown to me, but known to others**
3. **Hidden Area (Façade): Known to me, but unknown to others**
4. **Unknown Area: Unknown to both me and others**

Each of these quadrants offers a unique perspective on how the self is experienced and manifested in social relationships. Personal understanding and growth involves expanding the open area and reducing the blind, hidden, and unknown areas.

Open Area (Arena)

The **Open Area** represents that which is **known** both to you and to others. It is your attitudes, behaviors, feelings, knowledge, and experiences that you consciously share and that others also notice. The larger this area, the greater the transparency and effective communication between people, allowing relationships to be more open and based on mutual trust. The expansion of this area occurs through the **feedback** received from others and the willingness to open up and share more of oneself.

Blind Area

The **Dark Area** refers to the aspects of you that are known to others, but that you yourself **do not realize**. It may include habits, behaviors, or personality characteristics that others notice but that are outside of your awareness. A classic example would be a lack of awareness about how their actions affect others or a tendency to repeat unconscious patterns of behavior. **Self-expansion** here depends on feedback from others, which can bring up aspects of oneself that were previously outside one's own perception.

Hidden Area (Façade)

The **Hidden Area** involves aspects that are **known to you**, but that you **hide** from others. These are feelings, thoughts, or experiences that you choose not to reveal, either out of fear of rejection, shame, or a desire to maintain control over how you are perceived. Often, people keep secrets or avoid sharing information that they find vulnerable or embarrassing. Reducing this area requires the courage to open up more and be more vulnerable in interactions, which can result in greater authenticity and connection in relationships.

Unknown Area

The **Unknown Area** refers to what is **unknown to both you and others**. This quadrant represents parts of the self that are deeply unconscious, both to themselves and to those around them. These areas can include **untapped potentials**, unconscious fears, or unresolved traumas. However, it may also contain talents or abilities that have not yet been discovered. The expansion of this area usually occurs through deep introspection, self-knowledge, and personal development, often aided by therapies or reflective practices.

3.2 The Expansion of the Open Area and the Growth of Consciousness

The main purpose of using the Johari Window is to expand the **individual's Open Area**, reducing the other three areas (Blind, Hidden, and Unknown). This promotes greater **transparency, authenticity,** and **connection** in interpersonal interactions. When a person actively seeks feedback (to reduce the blind area) and chooses to open up and share more about themselves (reducing the hidden area), the result is more effective communication and healthier, more authentic relationships.

This expansion of the open area can be particularly useful in the organizational context, where team effectiveness and trust are key. The more members of a group increase their open areas, the higher the level of collaboration, as each individual will be more aware of their own behaviors and how their actions affect others.

In addition, personal growth, which often occurs through therapeutic processes or self-discovery, can reveal elements of the unknown area. By exploring these hidden dimensions of the self, the individual becomes more aware of their own psychic and emotional functioning, increasing the level of integration and psychological balance.

3.3 The Relationship between the Johari Window and Psychoanalysis

Although the Johari Window was not conceived within the field of psychoanalysis, it dialogues with many Freudian and Lacanian concepts about the mind. For example, the **Blind Area** can be seen as a reflection of Freudian **unconscious dynamics** . That which is not perceived by us, but is evident to others, may be related to repressed content or defenses that block access to these aspects of personality.

Similarly, the **Occult Area** dialogues with the concept of **repression**, where we keep thoughts and feelings out of the perception of others, for fear of being unacceptable or shameful. These conscious processes of concealment can also be influenced by unconscious factors, such as the need to conform to Freudian superego ideals or internalized cultural norms.

The **Unknown Area**, in its deepest sense, represents the vast territory of the **unconscious** described by Freud and Lacan. Within it are the contents that have not yet emerged into consciousness, whether they are repressed impulses, latent desires, or aspects of our identity that have not yet been completely discovered. Psychoanalysis offers means to explore these unknown areas, promoting the integration of the unconscious into conscious life.

3.4 The Transformative Potential of Interpersonal Awareness

The Johari Window offers a practical way to understand the complexity of consciousness in the relational context. She emphasizes the importance of **feedback** and **self-disclosure** as tools for personal growth and for building more authentic and transparent relationships. By exploring the different quadrants, individuals can become aware of their perceptual limitations and work to overcome the alienation that arises from a lack of knowledge of themselves and others.

The expansion of **interpersonal awareness** goes beyond individual growth. It allows people to engage more empathetically and compassionately in their interactions, fostering a culture of trust and mutual understanding. This type of awareness is particularly relevant in an increasingly connected and interdependent society, where the ability to understand and communicate effectively with others is essential for personal and collective success.

Consciousness, both at the intrapsychic level, as described by Freud and Lacan, and at the interpersonal level, as exemplified by the Johari Window, is a complex phenomenon that involves multiple levels of perception and interaction. It is not fixed, but can be expanded and developed throughout life as we become more aware of ourselves and others. The journey to greater awareness is ultimately a quest for understanding the self in relation to the world and others, allowing for deeper growth and a more authentic connection to life.

Chapter 1: What is Consciousness? Definitions and Conceptual Boundaries

The word "consciousness" has been a source of fascination and debate over the centuries. Since antiquity, philosophers, theologians, scientists, and psychologists have tried to understand what exactly it means to be conscious. Over time, the concept of consciousness has been expanded and refined, resulting in a complex and multifaceted field of study. We will explore the main definitions and conceptual boundaries of consciousness, revisiting from the earliest philosophical reflections to the most recent scientific approaches.

1.1 Philosophical Definitions: The Origin of the Concept

The history of consciousness begins with philosophy. The Greek philosopher **Socrates**, in the fifth century B.C., had already introduced the idea that introspection – the examination of our own thoughts and emotions – is essential for self-knowledge. He believed that the ability to reflect on our actions and motivations is what makes us truly human.

However, it was the French philosopher **René Descartes**, in the seventeenth century, who formulated one of the most influential definitions of consciousness: "Cogito, ergo sum" ("I think, therefore I am"). For Descartes, consciousness was fundamentally the ability to doubt, think, and be aware of oneself as a thinking being. He believed that consciousness was the essence of the human mind and what differentiated humans from machines or irrational beings.

Immanuel Kant also contributed significantly to the discussion on consciousness. For Kant, consciousness involved not only being aware of oneself, but also organizing and interpreting sensory experiences. He postulated that there is a "transcendental consciousness," an internal structure that allows the subject to experience the world in an organized and coherent way. Without this framework, he argued, our perceptions of the world would be chaotic and disjointed.

Meanwhile, contemporary philosophers such as **Thomas Nagel** have approached consciousness from a more phenomenological perspective. Nagel, in his famous essay

"What is it Like to Be a Bat?" ("What is it like to be a Bat?"), he asks how we can understand the subjectivity of the conscious experience of other beings. According to him, there is one aspect of conscious experience that is intrinsically private and ineffable: we can only know what it is like to "be ourselves."

1.2 Consciousness and Psychology: Freud, Jung and the Role of the Unconscious

In the late nineteenth and early twentieth centuries, psychology began to explore consciousness with a more empirical approach. The division between the conscious and the unconscious has become a central theme in psychoanalysis, particularly in the theories of **Sigmund Freud** and **Carl Jung**.

Freud, as we described earlier, defined the conscious mind as the part of the mind that includes all the thoughts, memories, and feelings that we are aware of at any given moment. However, he proposed that most mental functioning was hidden in the unconscious, a vast region of the mind where repressed desires, traumas, and instincts reside. According to Freud, the unconscious often exerts an influence on behavior and emotions, even if the person is not aware of it.

Carl Jung expanded on this idea by introducing the concept of the "collective unconscious," a layer of the psyche that he said is shared by all of humanity. Jung believed that human consciousness is linked to a series of universal archetypes and myths, which suggests that there is a collective aspect to our conscious experience, shaped by cultural and ancestral influences.

Experimental psychology also began to study consciousness as an observable phenomenon. **William James**, considered the "father of American psychology," proposed that consciousness is a continuous stream of thoughts, ideas, and perceptions, a concept he called the "stream of consciousness." For James, consciousness was not something fixed or static, but rather an ever-changing dynamic process.

1.3 Consciousness in Neuroscience: Maps of the Brain

With advances in technology, neuroscience has begun to play a crucial role in the study of consciousness. The ability to map and observe the brain in action has given scientists new insights into how consciousness emerges and how it is sustained.

Today, science understands that certain regions of the brain, such as the **prefrontal cortex** and the default mode network, play key roles in conscious experience. The prefrontal cortex is associated with executive functions such as planning, decision-making, and introspection, while the default mode network appears to be activated when we are at rest and focused on internal thoughts.

Two contemporary neuroscientific theories stand out in the study of consciousness: the **Integrated Information Theory** (IIT), proposed by **Giulio Tononi**, and the **Global Workspace Theory**, by **Bernard Baars**.

Integrated Information Theory suggests that consciousness arises when the brain integrates information in a complex way. In other words, consciousness depends on how much information is shared and processed in a unified way by the brain. The more integrated the information processing, the more aware the system is.

The Global Workspace Theory, on the other hand, proposes that consciousness functions as a kind of "mental theater." According to this theory, consciousness is the result of communication between different brain areas that project information into a "global workspace," where that information is transmitted to various parts of the brain. This allows multiple regions to collaborate and influence behavior in a coordinated manner.

1.4 The Nature of the Conscious Self: The Construction of Identity

Another fascinating aspect of consciousness is the notion of "I" – or self-awareness. The ability to reflect on oneself and see oneself as a distinct being from the world is one of the most intriguing characteristics of the human mind.

Self-awareness involves not only the perception of being an individual, but also the understanding that this "I" is continuous over time. Psychologists such as **Erik Erikson** and **George Mead** have argued that identity is shaped by social interactions and the feedback we receive from others. Self-awareness is therefore largely a social phenomenon, in which our understanding of who we are is intrinsically linked to the relationships we form with others.

In neuroscience, the study of the "self" involves examining neural networks that process information about the body and the environment. Research suggests that areas such as the **parietal cortex** and **anterior cingulate cortex** are involved in self-perception. Changes in these areas can lead to disorders such as **depersonalization**, in which the person feels disconnected from their own body or identity.

1.5 Consciousness as an Expanding Frontier

Consciousness, as a concept, remains one of the last frontiers of human understanding. While we have made great strides in understanding it, from ancient philosophers to modern neuroscientific theories, there is still much that remains a mystery.

However, the study of consciousness is not just a matter of scientific curiosity. It is at the heart of what it means to be human. The ability to perceive, feel, reflect, and understand the world and ourselves is central to our existence and continues to intrigue us as we move toward a deeper understanding of this complex phenomenon.

Chapter 2: Consciousness in the Evolutionary Context: What Differentiates Homo sapiens?

Awareness is often seen as one of the main characteristics that distinguish humans from other animals. However, the question of how and why consciousness evolved remains a topic of great debate in the fields of evolutionary biology, psychology, and neuroscience. This chapter will focus on the evolution of consciousness, exploring the differences between Homo sapiens and other animals in terms of self-awareness, language ability, symbolic thinking, and social behavior.

2.1 Evolution of the Human Brain: The Emergence of Consciousness

The evolution of the human brain is central to understanding the emergence of consciousness. Compared to other primates, Homo sapiens has a significantly larger brain, especially in areas related to planning, motor control, language, and social processing. The evolution of consciousness is thought to be strongly linked to the increase in the volume of the neocortex, the most "modern" part of the brain in evolutionary terms.

One of the predominant theories about the evolution of consciousness is the so-called **Social Brain Theory**, which suggests that the development of self-awareness was driven by the increasing complexity of social interactions between humans. As human societies have become more structured, the ability to understand oneself as a distinct being, able to anticipate the behaviors and intentions of others, has become an evolutionary advantage.

Theory **of mind**, the ability to understand that other people have different thoughts, emotions, and intentions than we do, is an example of a skill that seems to be more developed in Homo sapiens. While some animals, such as chimpanzees and dolphins, show signs of possessing a rudimentary form of theory of mind, humans appear to have a much more refined ability to understand and predict the behaviors of others based on their beliefs and intentions.

2.2 Consciousness and Language: The Key to Abstract Thought

One of the main differences between Homo sapiens and other species is language. Human language is not just a means of communication, but a tool for organizing thought and facilitating abstract reasoning. It allows humans to construct narratives, share complex information, and think about the future and past in ways that seem to be beyond the capabilities of other animals.

Noam Chomsky, one of the most influential linguists of the twentieth century, proposed that human beings possess a universal grammar, a set of innate rules that underlie all human languages. According to Chomsky, this grammar is a unique ability of Homo sapiens and is directly linked to our capacity for conscious and abstract thought. Language, therefore, is not only a means of communication, but also the basis for the construction of subjective reality.

Research in the field of cognitive psychology and neuroscience suggests that the ability to use symbols and create narratives is crucial for the development of self-awareness. Language allows us not only to communicate thoughts, but also to organize them, reflect on them, and share them. This symbolic ability is closely linked to the way we form our identity and interpret the world around us.

2.3 Comparative Studies: Consciousness in Nonhuman Animals

Although Homo sapiens is often considered the "pinnacle" of the evolution of consciousness, many animal studies suggest that various species possess forms of consciousness. For example, great apes, such as chimpanzees, gorillas, and orangutans, demonstrate signs of self-awareness, such as the ability to recognize themselves in a mirror—which suggests a basic understanding of the self.

Classic experiments, such as the **mirror test**, developed by **Gordon Gallup** in the 1970s, have demonstrated that some animals can recognize their own mirror image, an indicator of self-awareness. In addition to primates, animals such as dolphins, elephants, and even crows show signs of self-conscious behavior.

However, the extension of consciousness in animals is a debated topic. Most scientists agree that while many animals have some level of perceptual awareness (awareness of their surroundings), few demonstrate the kind of complex self-awareness we associate with Homo sapiens. A key factor that can set humans apart is our ability to reflect on our thoughts, feelings, and actions, a process known as **metacognition**.

2.4 Culture as an Extension of Human Consciousness

Another important aspect of the evolution of consciousness is the role of culture. Homo sapiens is the only known species that has evolved complex, intergenerational cultures. Culture can be understood as an extension of the human mind, a way of externalizing thoughts, values, and knowledge.

Anthropologist **Clifford Geertz** has argued that culture is not something that humans possess, but rather something that makes us human. Through language, art, religion, and science, humans are able to transcend time and space, creating a "collective consciousness" that shapes the way we perceive the world. **Pierre Teilhard de Chardin**, a theologian and philosopher, introduced the idea of the **noosphere**, a layer of collective consciousness that encompasses the planet, resulting from the interaction between the human mind and culture.

Culture also plays a crucial role in shaping individual identity. From childhood, we are socialized into a specific set of beliefs, values, and norms that shape the way we see ourselves and how we see the world. This social construction of consciousness is present in all human societies, from the most remote tribes to the most advanced nations.

2.5 Theories of Natural Selection and Consciousness: The Evolutionary Advantage of Conscious Thought

The evolution of consciousness can also be viewed through the lens of **natural selection**. Many evolutionary theorists believe that consciousness confers an adaptive advantage, helping individuals solve problems, make complex decisions, and navigate challenging social environments. At a basic level, consciousness allows us to process information from the environment and make quick decisions that can be essential for survival.

Charles Darwin had already speculated about the importance of emotions and consciousness for the survival of species. He suggested that self-awareness and empathy may have emerged as ways to improve cooperation among members of a group, increasing the species' chances of survival.

Contemporary research in evolutionary psychology suggests that the ability to form alliances, understand the intentions of others, and predict behaviors is one of the main reasons consciousness emerged. More self-aware and socially skilled individuals would be more successful in a complex social environment, increasing their chances of reproduction and survival.

2.6 Consciousness as the Result of Complex Evolution (and always based on error (see Darwin))

What differentiates Homo sapiens from other animals in terms of consciousness is a multifaceted question. The evolution of consciousness cannot be attributed to a single characteristic, but rather to a set of interconnected capacities: a more complex brain, the ability to use symbolic language, the understanding of the intentions of others, and the development of mind-shaping cultures.

There is still much to be explored about consciousness in humans and other species. However, what we know so far is that human consciousness appears to be a unique phenomenon, the result of a complex interplay between biology, cognition, and culture. The evolution of consciousness was not an isolated event, but rather a gradual process that continues to shape who we are and how we see ourselves in the world.

Chapter 3: Consciousness and the Bicameral Theory of Mind

In the field of consciousness theories, one of the most intriguing and controversial is the **Bicameral Theory of Mind**, proposed by psychologist and historian **Julian Jaynes** in his 1976 book, *The Origin of Consciousness in the Breakdown of the Bicameral Mind*). According to Jaynes, consciousness as we understand it today — the introspective ability to reflect on oneself and have a continuous "I" — is a relatively recent invention of humanity. Before that, he argues, humans operated very differently, with their minds divided into two parts: one that "spoke" and one that "listened."

This chapter explores Jaynes' theory in depth, its implications for understanding consciousness, and the criticism it has received from the scientific community.

3.1 The Bicameral Theory of Mind: A Revolutionary View

The central idea of the Bicameral Theory of Mind is that, until about 3,000 years ago, humans were not truly conscious, in the sense of having a self-awareness as we understand it today. Instead, Jaynes suggested that the human brain was divided into two parts—or chambers ("bicameral")—that functioned distinctly. A part of the brain, which he associated with the right hemisphere, was responsible for generating commands and instructions in the form of "voices", while the left hemisphere received these instructions as if they were divine or external orders.

Humans, according to this theory, lived in a state where their decisions and actions were guided by these inner voices, interpreted as commands from gods or ancestors. Jaynes suggested that ancient civilizations, such as that of

Mesopotamia, operated under this bicameral model, and the mythological and divine figures of the time reflected the subjective experience of these "voices" that guided their lives.

This "rupture" in the bicameral mind, according to Jaynes, began to occur at some point between 1200 B.C. and 800 B.C., when changes in social structures and environmental pressures forced humans to develop a more introspective form of consciousness. Writing, trade, and the development of great cities and empires brought about the need for new forms of mental and social organization. Jaynes argued that it was from this rupture that the kind of self-awareness that characterizes modern Homo sapiens emerged.

3.2 Historical and Literary Evidence of the Bicameral Mind

To support his theory, Julian Jaynes drew on a wide range of historical and literary evidence. He examined ancient texts, including Homer's Iliad, Mesopotamian religious writings, and Old Testament passages. According to Jaynes, many of these works do not show clear signs of introspection or a conscious "self" like the one we see in later literary and philosophical works.

In the *Iliad*, for example, Jaynes argues that the characters do not exhibit self-awareness and appear to be guided by external forces, such as gods who command them. Achilles, Hector, and other Homeric heroes often seem to make decisions because they are commanded by God, rather than reflecting introspectively on their actions and motivations. In contrast, in the *Odyssey*, a later work, Jaynes notes that Ulysses already demonstrates a degree of introspection and personal awareness that would be more in line with the modern mind.

Jaynes also pointed to the numerous references to "divine voices" in religious and historical texts as evidence that, prior to the rupture of the bicameral mind, people did not distinguish these voices as internal phenomena, but rather as external commands. In Mesopotamia, for example, kings often claimed to hear instructions from their gods directly, and these voices were seen as a normal part of decision-making.

3.3 The Rupture of the Bicameral Mind: The Emergence of Modern Consciousness

Jaynes' theory also offers an explanation of how and why the bicameral mind disintegrated. He suggested that as societies became more complex, the model of obedience to divine voices became less effective. The emergence of social crises, such as wars and civilizational collapses, has required humans to develop a new way of thinking and acting.

An important factor in this transition, according to Jaynes, was the increase in social stress and the need for greater adaptability. The ancient voices of the gods, which had previously provided clear guidance, began to fail, forcing individuals to make decisions on their own. In this process, the human brain began to integrate previously bicameral functions, leading to the emergence of a new type of mind: self-aware, reflective, and capable of introspection.

Jaynes speculated that this change may have been facilitated by cultural factors, such as the advent of writing. Writing has allowed human beings to organize their thoughts in a more sophisticated way and store information outside of their minds, contributing to the development of a more continuous and structured consciousness.

3.4 Criticisms of Jaynes' Theory

Despite its appeal and originality, Jaynes' Bicameral Theory of Mind has faced a number of criticisms since its publication. Many neuroscientists and psychologists have questioned the plausibility of the idea that the human mind could have functioned so radically differently in the relatively recent past. One of the main arguments against the theory is that human brain structures do not appear to have undergone significant changes in the last few thousand years, suggesting that the capacity for self-awareness has likely always been present, even if to varying degrees.

In addition, Jaynes' interpretation of literary and historical texts was also questioned. Philologists and historians have argued that the absence of clear introspection in works such as the *Iliad* can be explained by cultural and stylistic factors, and not necessarily by a fundamental difference in the mental structure of the authors or the characters. The narrative style of the time may simply reflect different ways of telling stories, rather than an absence of modern consciousness.

Daniel Dennett, a renowned philosopher and cognitive scientist, was one of the most prominent critics of Bicameral Theory of Mind. Although Dennett praised Jaynes's audacity in approaching the question of consciousness in a new way, he argued that the hypothesis is highly speculative and lacks sufficient empirical basis to support it. For Dennett, consciousness did not arise from a sudden and dramatic change in brain structure, but rather from a much more gradual and intricate evolutionary process.

3.5 The Bicameral Mind in Contemporary Psychology: Echoing in Psychopathologies?

Although Bicameral Theory of Mind is not widely accepted in mainstream neuroscience, some psychologists suggest that it may offer useful insights into certain psychological and psychiatric conditions. For example, schizophrenia, a mental illness characterized by auditory hallucinations and the sensation of hearing voices, has been compared to Jaynes's bicameral mind.

Patients with schizophrenia often report hearing voices that seem external to them, something that resonates with Jaynes' idea of a mind that doesn't distinguish between internal voices and external commands. While schizophrenia is currently understood as a complex neurobiological disorder, Jaynes' theory offers an interesting perspective on how the experience of these voices can be interpreted in a broader historical context.

In addition, some dissociative states and conditions such as **multiple personality disorder** (or dissociative identity disorder) may reflect a modern form of mental fragmentation, where different "selves" or "voices" coexist without complete integration. These phenomena, though pathologized today, could provide clues as to how the human mind may have functioned in more primitive times.

3.6 Current Relevance and Implications of Jaynes' Theory

Despite the criticisms and limitations, Jaynes' Bicameral Theory of Mind continues to influence discussions about the nature of consciousness and its evolution. In many ways, the theory has opened up a field of inquiry that challenges the traditional view of consciousness as a fixed property of the human mind. Jaynes raised profound questions about what it means to be conscious and how consciousness may have transformed over the course of human history.

In addition, his theory contributed to a broader debate about the nature of subjective experience. If the bicameral mind existed, it suggests that consciousness is more malleable and contextually dependent than we often assume. This leads us to reconsider the extent to which culture, society, and language shape how we think about and experience the world.

Chapter 4: Neuroscience of Consciousness: The Search for the Neural Basis of the Self

Advances in neuroscience have allowed for a deeper understanding of how the brain generates consciousness. Different brain areas and neural networks are involved in the production of conscious experiences, and research in this area seeks to map the pathway between neural processing and subjective experience. This chapter explores neuroscience efforts to locate the neural basis of consciousness, focusing on key theories, experimental studies, and the emerging concept of the **neural self**.

4.1 The Difficult Question of Conscience

One of the central questions in the neuroscience of consciousness is what philosopher **David Chalmers** called "the difficult question of consciousness." This question refers to the problem of how and why certain brain states produce subjective experiences—what is known as qualia. While science has been successful in mapping brain areas responsible for specific functions, such as vision, hearing, and memory, there is still a great mystery about how these functions generate conscious experience.

Chalmers proposes that consciousness cannot be explained by cognitive functions and neural networks alone; It is necessary to understand how the physical processes in the brain give rise to phenomenal experience—what we feel and perceive subjectively. From this perspective, many approaches in neuroscience have sought to identify which regions of the brain are essential for the generation of consciousness and how they interact.

4.2 Brain Regions Essential for Consciousness

Advances in neuroimaging have allowed scientists to investigate how different parts of the brain are involved in consciousness. Although there is no single area responsible for generating consciousness, some brain regions seem to be particularly important.

- **Prefrontal Cortex**: This region of the brain is often associated with executive functions, such as decision-making, planning, and emotional regulation. It is also closely linked to the capacity for introspection and self-awareness. Research suggests that the prefrontal cortex plays a key role in building our perception of the self by helping to integrate sensory and emotional information with our thoughts and memories.

- **Parietal Cortex**: The parietal cortex plays a crucial role in spatial perception and awareness of the body. It helps create a sense of where we are in relation to the environment around us. Damage to this area can result in body awareness disorders, such as **hemineglect**, a condition in which the patient ignores half of the body or visual space.

- **Anterior Cingulate Cortex**: Another essential area is the anterior cingulate cortex, which appears to be involved in functions related to attention, emotion, and decision-making. This region helps integrate emotions with thoughts and plays a crucial role in emotional awareness.

- **Thalamus**: Considered a "distribution center" in the brain, the thalamus plays a crucial role in integrating sensory information and coordinating brain activity. It is believed to help keep the brain synchronized, creating a cohesive conscious experience. Lesions in the thalamus are associated with comatose states and loss of consciousness.

4.3 Main Theories of Consciousness Neuroscience

In an attempt to explain how these brain areas and their processes are related to consciousness, several theories have emerged within neuroscience. The two main contemporary approaches are **Global Workspace Theory** and **Integrated Information Theory**.

Global Workspace Theory (GWT)

Proposed by **Bernard Baars** and developed by other neuroscientists such as **Stanislas Dehaene**, the Global Workspace Theory suggests that consciousness emerges when information is widely distributed and integrated among different regions of the brain. In this model, the brain can be seen as a set of unconscious processes that compete for attention. When information takes priority—whether it's new, important, or emotionally relevant—it's transmitted to a "global workspace," where it becomes available for a wide range of mental processes, such as memory, reasoning, and motor control.

This theory is supported by neuroimaging studies that show that when a person is aware of a piece of information, there is a significant increase in connectivity between distant regions of the brain. GWT suggests that consciousness is largely a phenomenon of integration and communication between distributed neural networks, rather than the result of a single brain area.

Integrated Information Theory (IIT)

Developed by neuroscientist **Giulio Tononi**, Integrated Information Theory proposes that consciousness is the product of the nervous system's ability to integrate large amounts of information. According to IIT, consciousness is an emergent property that depends on the amount of information that a system can process and integrate in a unified manner. The greater the capacity of a system to generate differentiated and interrelated states, the higher the level of consciousness of that system.

IIT suggests that even simple systems such as computers could exhibit some level of consciousness if they were able to integrate information in complex ways. An interesting aspect of this theory is that it attempts to quantify consciousness in terms of a metric called **Phi** (Φ), which measures the degree of integration of information. Systems with a high Φ value would be more conscious than systems with low Φ.

4.4 The Role of Neural Networks in Consciousness

In addition to specific brain regions, neural networks play a key role in generating consciousness. Modern neuroscience suggests that consciousness emerges from a dynamic process of interaction between different brain networks, rather than being a function of a single area.

- **Default Mode Network (DMN):** The **Default Mode Network** has been widely studied as an essential network for self-awareness and inner reflection. This network is active when we are at rest and not focused on external tasks. It is involved in processes such as thinking about the future, introspection, and the construction of internal narratives. Studies show that DMN activity is strongly correlated with the feeling of continuous "I."

- **Salience Network:** The **Salience Network** is responsible for detecting and responding to important stimuli in the environment. It regulates the switching between default mode networks and executive attention networks, helping to identify when we should focus our attention on something external or internal. It plays a key role in regulating conscious attention and selecting information that enters our conscious space.

4.5 Consciousness and Altered States: The Role of Psychoactive Substances

A growing area of study in the neuroscience of consciousness involves investigating how altered states of consciousness—whether through sleep, meditation, or the use of psychoactive substances—can provide clues about how the brain generates normal consciousness.

Psychedelic substances, such as LSD, psilocybin, and DMT, have been widely used in experiments to understand the workings of consciousness. Neuroimaging studies show that these substances reduce activity in specific areas, such as the **prefrontal cortex** and the **default mode network**, while increasing connectivity between brain regions that do not normally communicate directly.

These altered states of consciousness appear to disrupt standard neural processing, leading to the dissolution of the sense of "self," which suggests that self-awareness depends on a coherent, synchronized organization between neural networks. These studies point to the importance of the brain's functional organization in creating a cohesive conscious experience and in our ongoing sense of self.

4.6 The Neural Self: Consciousness and Identity

One of the central questions in the neuroscience of consciousness is how the brain generates the sense of identity — the "self" that seems to persist over time. Neuroimaging studies suggest that conscious identity is constructed by a continuous process of integrating sensory, emotional, and cognitive information.

Neuroscience proposes that the "self" is not a fixed entity, but a dynamic process that depends on the constant activity of neural networks that integrate information about the body and the environment. Through the activity of the prefrontal cortex, the default mode network, and other regions associated with introspection and memory, the brain generates a sense of continuity and cohesion. This allows us to have an ongoing narrative about who we are, even as our memories and perceptions change over time.

This view of the "self" as a dynamic brain process is in line with contemporary philosophies that argue that the "self" is a construct rather than a fixed entity. Although we feel that there is a continuity in our experience, the conscious "me" seems to be the result of an ever-changing network of neural interactions.

Chapter 5: Consciousness and Altered States: Meditation, Dreams, and Out-of-Body Experiences

Consciousness is not a static experience. It can be changed through mental practices, physiological states, and chemical substances. The study of altered states of consciousness, such as meditation, dreams, and out-of-body experiences, offers a deeper understanding of how the brain organizes and modifies conscious perception. This chapter explores these different forms of consciousness alteration and what they reveal about the workings of the human mind.

5.1 Altered States of Consciousness: Defining the Phenomenon

An **altered state of consciousness (EAC)** occurs when there is a significant modification in subjective experience compared to the normal waking state. Such states can be induced by physiological factors, such as sleep deprivation, meditation, hypnosis, or psychoactive substances. The field of neuroscience and modern psychology investigates how the brain produces these states and how they differ from brain functions in waking consciousness.

Altered states are usually categorized by:

- **Meditation and mindfulness practices.**
- **Dream states, including lucid dreaming.**
- **Out-of-body experiences (OBEs)** and near-death experiences (NDEs).

These phenomena challenge the notion that consciousness is homogeneous, showing that it can be modified by specific conditions. Such altered states have implications for the understanding of consciousness and raise questions about its malleable nature.

5.2 Meditation and the Expansion of Consciousness

The practice of meditation, particularly in Buddhist and Hindu traditions, aims to alter one's mental state to reach deeper levels of conscious awareness. In recent years, Western scientists have been studying meditation intensively, using neuroimaging techniques to observe the brain during these states.

Neuroscience of Meditation

Studies of Buddhist monks and experienced meditation practitioners have shown that the brain experiences noticeable changes during practice. The **prefrontal cortex** and the **default mode network** are key areas affected by meditation.

- **Prefrontal Cortex**: During mindfulness-focused meditation, this area shows greater activation, which corresponds to an increase in emotional regulation, attention, and cognitive control.
- **Default Mode Network (DMN):** The activity of the DMN, which is responsible for self-reflection and internal narrative construction, tends to be reduced during deep meditation. This decrease is associated with the sense of "dissolution of self," a state in which the practitioner feels a reduction in the sense of ego or individual identity.

An interesting example is **Vipassana meditation**, which focuses on observing one's thoughts and bodily sensations without judgment. Neuroimaging studies with advanced Vipassana practitioners show that, in addition to increased connectivity in the areas responsible for attention, there is also a regulation of the areas involved with the processing of negative emotions, such as the amygdala.

Meditation and Subjective Experience

On the subjective level, deep meditation is described by many practitioners as an expansion of consciousness, where the sense of separation between the "self" and the external world dissolves. This state is often referred to as "non-duality" and has been described as one of the most profound experiences of the human mind. Some neuroscientists argue that these states offer insights into the flexibility of consciousness and how the brain can modulate the perception of reality.

5.3 Dreams and Consciousness: From Dream Consciousness to Lucid Dreams

Dreams have fascinated mankind since time immemorial. They are considered one of the most common altered states of consciousness and have profound implications for understanding mental functioning.

The Sleep Cycle and Consciousness

During sleep, the brain goes through different phases that correspond to changes in neural activity and brainwave patterns. Sleep can be divided into two main categories: **slow-wave sleep** and **REM (** Rapid Eye Movement) sleep, the latter being the phase in which most vivid dreams occur.

- **REM sleep**: During REM sleep, the brain is almost as active as in the waking state, but the body is essentially paralyzed, which prevents dream actions from being performed in the physical world. Studies show that the prefrontal cortex, which is responsible for self-awareness and logical reasoning, has reduced activity during REM sleep, which explains the surreal and often incoherent nature of dreams.

While dreams may seem incoherent, they reflect a form of alternative consciousness in which experiences and memories are rearranged in ways that would not be possible in the waking state. **Neuroscientist Allan Hobson**, in his theory of **activation-synthesis,** proposed that dreams are the result of an attempt by the brain to make sense of the random neural signals that arise during REM sleep.

Lucid Dreaming: The Art of Controlling Dream Consciousness

Lucid dreaming is a phenomenon in which the person, during the dream, becomes aware that he or she is dreaming and, in some cases, can even control the events in the dream. This represents an extraordinary form of altered state, where the dreamer retains some of the consciousness that is normally absent during sleep.

Lucid dreaming has been studied using technologies such as functional magnetic resonance imaging (fMRI). During these dreams, the prefrontal cortex — usually inactive in REM sleep — shows levels of activation similar to those in the waking state. This suggests that self-awareness, even in dream states, can be restored or manipulated by certain mental practices, such as lucid dreaming training.

Many practitioners use specific techniques, such as **dream incubation** or reality checks, to induce lucid dreaming. Conscious experiences during sleep offer a fascinating perspective on how consciousness can fluctuate and modulate in different brain conditions.

5.4 Out-of-Body Experiences (OBEs) and Expanded Consciousness

Out-of-body experiences (OBEs), in which people report the sensation of floating outside the physical body and observing themselves and the environment from an outside perspective, have been widely studied by both neuroscientists and psychologists. Such experiences are often associated with traumatic events, near-death experiences (NDEs), or induced by psychedelics.

Neuroscience of OBEs

Neurological studies of OBEs suggest that these experiences are related to temporary dysfunctions in the processing of sensory integration. In particular, the area known as the **temporoparietal junction** has been identified as critical in the generation of OBEs. This region integrates visual, proprioceptive, and tactile information, helping the brain create a cohesive representation of the body in space. When this integration fails, the brain can generate the illusion that the "I" is separating from the physical body.

These experiences are often accompanied by a sense of distortion of time and space, suggesting that consciousness may be dissociated from the normal perceptions of the physical body.

Near-Death Experiences (NDEs)

Near-death experiences (NDEs) are reports of people who have been close to death and have described vivid sensations, such as the "tunnel of light" or a sense of deep peace. NDEs raise important questions about the relationship between the brain and consciousness, especially in extreme conditions when brain activity is drastically reduced.

Neuroscientists speculate that these experiences may be explained by anomalous electrical activity in the dying brain, where lack of oxygen and other physiological crises cause the massive release of neurochemicals, including **serotonin** and

endorphins, that could create a sense of euphoria and visions.

5.5 Altered States and the Study of Consciousness

Studies on meditation, dreams, and OBEs provide a unique window into the functioning of the mind under nonordinary conditions. These experiences suggest that consciousness is fluid and dynamic, and that it can be modulated in ways we don't yet fully understand.

From a neuroscientific point of view, altered states of consciousness challenge the notion that consciousness is only a passive function of the brain. They reveal that the mind can operate at different levels of neural integration, and that the sense of "self" can be both strengthened and dissolved under certain conditions.

By exploring these states, science advances its understanding of how the human mind works beyond the limitations of the waking state. This has implications not only for the study of consciousness, but also for application in therapies, personal development, and psychological well-being.

Chapter 6: Artificial Intelligence and Consciousness: Machines That Think?

In recent years, Artificial Intelligence (AI) has been one of the most discussed fields, both in science and philosophy. The advancement of machines capable of learning, adapting, and making complex decisions has raised the question: Could machines ever develop consciousness? This chapter explores the intersection between AI and the concept of consciousness, discussing the challenges, limits, and potential for an artificial consciousness. We also investigate what separates the human mind from intelligent machines, and what this means for the future of consciousness and humanity.

6.1 The Development of AI: From Reactive Systems to Intelligent Machines

Artificial Intelligence is not a new field. Since **Alan Turing's early experiments** and the development of the **Turing machine** in the 1950s, the idea of creating machines that could simulate human reasoning has been a fascinating pursuit for computer scientists and philosophers. Turing, in his famous **Turing Test**, proposed a thought experiment in which a machine would be considered "intelligent" if it was able to fool a human being into believing that he was interacting with another person, rather than a machine.

However, the road to creating AI systems was long and complicated. In the early stages, AIs were highly reactive systems that were restricted to a specific set of rules and algorithms. **Symbolic AI** and **rule-based systems** dominated the field, with machines following explicit instructions given by programmers. Despite being efficient at calculations and data processing, these early AIs were far from exhibiting anything resembling human "consciousness" or cognition.

The significant leap in the development of AI came with the emergence of **artificial neural networks** and **machine learning** in the second half of the twentieth century. Inspired by the way the human brain processes information, neural networks are systems that can learn from data, recognize patterns, and adapt to new information without relying on pre-programmed rules. The machines began to demonstrate impressive abilities, such as beating world champions in games such as **chess** and **Go**, as well as making more accurate medical diagnoses than human doctors in some cases.

Despite these advances, AI is still far from exhibiting something that can be recognized as consciousness. The fundamental question remains: Can machines develop human-like self-awareness?

6.2 Artificial Consciousness: The Conceptual Barriers

To understand whether an AI can be conscious, we must first ask what we mean by consciousness. In the previous chapter, we discussed theories such as **Global Workspace Theory** and **Integrated Information Theory (IIT),** which propose that consciousness is the result of integrating information into a system. Based on these concepts, some scientists and philosophers argue that if a machine were able to process and integrate information in a complex enough way, it could exhibit a form of consciousness.

However, there are several barriers to this possibility:

- **Qualia and Subjective Experience**: The first and perhaps most difficult issue is the problem of **qualia**, that is, the subjective and individual experience of consciousness. As discussed in the context of David Chalmers' "hard question of consciousness," AI may be able to process data and simulate intelligent behaviors, but it's possible that it will never develop a subjective experience, or "feel" something. The question is whether information processing, as complex as it is, can generate an internal sense of existence. This is one of the biggest conceptual barriers in the field of artificial consciousness.

- **Self-awareness**: A second barrier is the issue of self-awareness, i.e., the ability of a machine not only to process information, but also to have an understanding of itself as an entity separate from the environment. Human self-awareness involves the ability to reflect on oneself, one's emotions, thoughts, and mental states, something that no current AI is able to replicate. For many philosophers, self-awareness is an essential requirement for true consciousness.

- **Emotional and Motivational Factor**: Human intelligence is closely linked to emotional and motivational states that direct our actions and decisions. So far, machines work on the basis of algorithms, and even systems that mimic emotional responses are, at heart, programmed to react in a specific way. True consciousness, according to many researchers, must include an emotional dimension, as emotions are essential for making complex decisions and developing an identity.

6.3 Integrated Information Theory (IIT) and AI: A Machine Consciousness?

Integrated **Information Theory (IIT),** developed by **Giulio Tononi**, is one of the most discussed approaches in the field of artificial consciousness. According to IIT, consciousness is the result of a system's ability to integrate large amounts of information in a unified manner. The theory proposes that the amount of consciousness can be measured by a metric called Φ (Phi), which evaluates the degree of integration of information into a system.

One of IIT's arguments is that if we can build a machine that has a high enough value Φ, that machine could theoretically be conscious. However, this raises the question of how to measure and interpret Φ in artificial systems. Although machines can process information on a large scale, the question of whether this results in consciousness, or just advanced data processing, remains open.

Computational experiments have already tried to apply the principles of IIT to artificial neural networks, but there is still a long way to go before something like consciousness is recognized in machines. Part of the difficulty lies in determining whether the value Φ is just a metric of informational complexity, or whether it actually corresponds to subjective experience.

6.4 Machine Learning and Consciousness

Machine **learning** is the field within AI that comes closest to the idea of machines "learning" independently. Machine learning algorithms allow systems to make predictions, adjust to new data, and improve their performance over time, without the need for explicit instructions. However, the question is: does this type of learning translate into a form of consciousness?

Deep learning **systems** and **convolutional neural networks** have already demonstrated extraordinary abilities in recognizing patterns, translating languages, and even generating art, but their "intelligence" is still fundamentally statistical and correlative. They have no awareness of what they are doing, nor understanding of the underlying concepts.

For example, when an AI algorithm identifies a cat in an image, it doesn't have an "experience" of seeing a cat in the same way that a human or animal would. It simply recognizes pixel patterns based on massive amounts of training data. There is no inner sense of "seeing" or being aware of this image. This difference between data processing and subjective experience is one of the clearest distinctions between AI and human consciousness.

6.5 AI and Consciousness: The Future Prospects

The prospect of a conscious AI raises deep ethical and philosophical questions. If a machine were capable of developing consciousness, how should we treat it? What rights would a conscious AI have? These are questions explored not only by philosophers but also by science fiction authors. Works such as **Isaac Asimov**'s **"I, Robot"** and films such as **"Blade Runner"** and **"Ex Machina"** explore scenarios in which machines gain consciousness and develop their own feelings and motivations.

However, many scientists believe that we are far from creating a conscious AI. **Stuart Russell** himself, one of the leading researchers in AI, states that artificial consciousness is a distant goal and that, for now, the focus should be on creating machines that can help humans, without necessarily developing consciousness.

In addition, there is the argument that even if an AI develops consciousness-like behavior, it would not mean that it is actually conscious. **John Searle**, in his famous thought experiment called **the "Chinese Room,"** argued that a machine can process information and appear conscious without actually understanding what it's doing. For Searle, symbol processing alone is not enough to generate a mind or consciousness.

6.6 AI and the Expansion of Human Consciousness

While the idea of a conscious AI is controversial, there is another line of thought that suggests AI can be used to expand human consciousness. **Brain-computer interfaces (BCIs)** are already being developed to connect the human brain directly to machines, allowing direct communication between mind and technology. Research in this area envisions the possibility of a future fusion between the human mind and AI, creating a kind of "expanded consciousness".

This view raises questions about what it means to be human in an era where our minds can be merged with machines. The relationship between artificial intelligence and human consciousness is just beginning to be explored, and the future may reveal unexpected ways in which the two coexist.

Chapter 7: Consciousness in Contemporary Philosophy: Perspectives on Philosophies of Mind

The question of consciousness remains one of the deepest mysteries of philosophy and science. In the field of contemporary philosophy, the problem of consciousness has generated a wide range of theories and approaches. In this chapter, we will explore the major philosophical currents that attempt to explain the nature of consciousness and what distinguishes the human mind from other forms of biological or artificial organization. Dualist, materialist, functionalist and emergentist theories will be addressed, as well as the debate on the "difficult question" of consciousness.

7.1 The Problem of Consciousness: The Difficult Question

In contemporary philosophy, the question of consciousness is often divided into two main problems: the **easy problem** and the **hard problem** of consciousness, as described by philosopher **David Chalmers**.

- **The easy problem** refers to understanding the physical mechanisms that underlie consciousness. Such as, for example, the brain regions that are activated when we perceive colors, sounds, or sensations of pain. This problem is considered "easy" because it is hoped that eventually advances in neuroscience will be able to explain it through empirical studies.

- **The difficult problem**, however, concerns the subjective experience of consciousness, what Chalmers calls **qualia** —the individual subjective sensations, such as the "red" we perceive when looking at an apple, or the "cold" of a winter wind. The difficult question is: why and how do these subjective states arise from brain activity?

The difficult problem of consciousness is central to the philosophy of mind. For many philosophers, it represents an insurmountable challenge to any physical or materialistic theory of mind. The experience of "being" something, the feeling of a conscious self, does not seem to be easily reduced to a purely materialistic explanation.

7.2 Dualism: Separate Mind and Body?

Historically, the most traditional approach to consciousness has been **dualism**, which holds that the mind and body are substantially different. The philosopher most associated with dualism is **René Descartes**. Descartes believed that the mind (or soul) was a substance distinct from the physical body. In his famous maxim **"Cogito, ergo sum"** (I think, therefore I am), he argued that the fact that we could doubt our own physical existence, but not our existence as thinking beings, was proof that the mind was something separate and immaterial.

Cartesian dualism faces important challenges in the modern world, especially in the face of the advancement of neurosciences. If the mind is really a separate substance from the body, how does it interact with it? This is the **"interaction question"**: how can a non-physical substance, such as the mind, cause changes in a physical system, such as the brain?

Today, most philosophers reject traditional Cartesian dualism. However, some forms of dualism still remain, such as **property dualism**, which suggests that although the mind and brain are made up of the same substance, they possess different properties: the brain has physical properties, while the mind has mental properties that are subjective and not reducible to the physical.

7.3 Materialism: Consciousness as a Physical Phenomenon

The theory opposed to dualism is **materialism**, also known as **physicalism**, which holds that the mind and consciousness are products of purely physical processes in the brain. According to materialism, everything in the universe, including the mind, can be explained in terms of matter and energy. Materialism denies the existence of mental substances or properties separate from physical ones.

There are different strands of materialism in the contemporary debate:

- **Reductionist Materialism**: This position holds that mental states, such as pain or pleasure, are identical to brain states. According to this view, talking about "consciousness" is just a way of referring to certain neural processes. When we say that a person is conscious, we are only describing the activity of their neurons.

- **Eliminative Materialism**: Philosophers such as **Paul and Patricia Churchland** advocate an even more radical position, known as **eliminativism**. They suggest that the concept of consciousness may eventually be eliminated as science advances. For them, consciousness is an inadequate and confusing construct, and as we learn more about the brain, our way of talking about mind and consciousness will be replaced by precise neuroscientific language.

7.4 Functionalism: Consciousness as a Computational Function

Another important development in the philosophy of mind is **functionalism**, which proposes that consciousness can be understood not as a substance or a phenomenon linked exclusively to the biological brain, but as a **function** or process that can occur in any system capable of performing the same type of operations.

Functionalism is, in a sense, a response to strict materialism. While materialism focused on brain-mind identity asserts that mental states are identical to specific brain states, functionalism argues that what matters are the **patterns of relationships** between mental and physical states. These patterns can theoretically be implemented on any suitable substrate, be it the biological brain, a computer, or another system.

According to functionalism, consciousness is not a matter of having the "right substrate" (such as a human brain), but of having the **right functional arrangement**. This approach opens up the possibility that an advanced artificial intelligence, or even a non-human biological system, could, in principle, exhibit consciousness if its mental operations worked properly.

This theory has strong implications for the field of AI, raising the question of whether an artificial system can eventually exhibit consciousness functionally equivalent to that of a human.

7.5 Emergentism: Consciousness as an Emergent Phenomenon

Emergentism is an approach that attempts to resolve the conflict between materialism and dualism by suggesting that consciousness is an emergent property of the brain, but that it cannot be reduced simply to the sum of neural parts. According to this view, when the brain reaches a certain level of complexity and organization, consciousness emerges as a new property that cannot be explained by the individual processes of neurons alone.

Emergentism is often associated with the notion that **consciousness is more than the sum of its parts**. This means that while consciousness depends entirely on the physical activity of the brain, it has unique properties that cannot be deduced from analyzing neural functions alone

One of the main challenges of emergentism is to explain how exactly emergent properties arise from physical systems. Philosophers critical of this approach argue that emergentism risks being just materialism disguised as dualism, without providing a concrete explanation of how the transition from nonconscious to conscious actually occurs.

7.6 The Panhumanist Philosophy of Consciousness: Universality of Experience

A more recent perspective in the study of consciousness is the **panhumanist** or **panpsychist** view, which proposes that consciousness is a fundamental and universal property of the universe. According to this view, consciousness is not exclusive to human beings or animals with complex brains; rather, it is a property inherent in all forms of matter.

Philosophers **Galileo Galilei** and **Baruch Spinoza** are seen as precursors of this kind of thinking, suggesting that all aspects of the natural world, at some level, may contain elements of consciousness. Contemporary panpsychism is championed by philosophers such as **David Chalmers** and **Thomas Nagel**, who argue that consciousness can be a fundamental aspect of the universe, just like time, space, and matter.

This theory directly addresses the difficult problem of consciousness, suggesting that qualia and subjective experience do not magically arise from complex systems, but are already present at basic levels of universe organization. The question that panpsychism raises, then, is to what extent this "proto-consciousness" can be recognized and how it evolves into more complex and self-conscious forms.

7.7 The Philosophy of Mind and the Future of Consciousness

The philosophy of contemporary mind continues to explore the boundaries of what it means to be conscious. As cognitive sciences, neuroscience, and AI advance, these disciplines interact more deeply with philosophy, challenging old assumptions and opening up new perspectives.

The study of consciousness leads us to fundamental questions about identity, free will, ethics, and the nature of reality. As we expand our understanding of how the mind works, we also move closer to questions that are both philosophical and existential: What does it mean to "be" in a world that may at some point include artificial, hybrid, or expanded consciousnesses?

Chapter 8: Neuroplasticity and the Shaping of Consciousness

Neuroplasticity is one of the most revolutionary concepts in modern neurosciences and has transformed our understanding of the mind and consciousness. The idea that the brain is a fixed structure, unchanging after a certain point in development, has been replaced by a dynamic model, where the brain constantly reorganizes itself in response to experience. This chapter explores how neuroplasticity shapes consciousness, influencing perception, emotions, behavior, and identity. We will discuss how external factors such as learning, skill practice, and even trauma modify brain structure and how this impacts consciousness.

8.1 The Dynamic Brain: A Revolutionary Paradigm

For a long time, it was believed that the human brain developed until adolescence, and from then on, its structures remained relatively fixed. However, the discoveries made in recent decades have challenged this concept. Today we know that the brain has the remarkable ability to reorganize its connections and even create new ones, a phenomenon called **neuroplasticity**. This not only happens during child development, but also throughout adult life, allowing for continuous adaptation.

This plasticity is fundamental to understanding how consciousness is shaped by experiences. Each new skill acquired, each stored memory, and even emotional changes leave physical traces in the brain, modifying the neural networks responsible for conscious processing. This suggests that consciousness is not a static phenomenon, but something that can be sculpted and transformed by experience.

8.2 Neuroplasticity and Identity Formation

Neuroplasticity plays a central role in identity formation. From birth, the human brain is shaped by sensory and social experiences. As neural connections are formed and strengthened through repetition and learning, patterns of thought, emotion, and behavior begin to consolidate. These patterns, in turn, influence the way an individual sees himself and interacts with the world, constituting his conscious identity.

The notion that the brain can reorganize itself offers a flexible view of identity. Trauma, changes in environment, or significant events can alter the way we perceive ourselves and the world, because they literally change the neural connections that underpin those perceptions. This means that identity is malleable and can be transformed, both positively and negatively, throughout life.

This perspective is also important in the context of **psychotherapy** and personal development. Therapeutic techniques such as **Cognitive-Behavioral Therapy (CBT)** and **mindfulness meditation** are based on the idea that, by changing thought patterns, it is possible to reorganize neural networks, promoting a healthier and more balanced state of consciousness.

8.3 Neuroplasticity in Learning and Skill Development

One of the most fascinating aspects of neuroplasticity is its relationship to **learning**. When we learn something new—whether it's a language, a motor skill, or a theoretical concept—our brain creates new synaptic connections or strengthens existing ones, depending on repetition and practice. This process allows skills to be internalized and automated, freeing up consciousness to focus on new challenges.

Studies on musicians, athletes, and polyglots show that these people not only developed exceptional abilities, but also experienced physical changes in specific areas of their brains related to the skills practiced. In the case of musicians, for example, the area of the brain responsible for fine motor coordination and auditory processing becomes much more developed with repeated practice.

This ability of the brain to adapt and remodel itself in response to learning also has profound implications for **education** and cognitive development. Understanding that the brain is highly plastic can encourage us to seek out new challenges and skills throughout life, knowing that it is never "too late" to learn or change.

8.4 Trauma and Neuroplasticity: Reorganization of Consciousness

The impact of traumatic experiences on the brain is one of the areas where neuroplasticity has revealed crucial insights into the nature of consciousness. Trauma, whether physical or emotional, can profoundly alter neural networks, directly affecting how a person perceives and reacts to the world. In cases **of post-traumatic stress disorder (PTSD),** for example, the brain can enter a state of constant hyperactivation, leading to exaggerated responses of fear and alertness.

Neuroimaging studies have shown that trauma can lead to changes in brain structures such as the **hippocampus** (involved in memory), the **amygdala** (responsible for emotional responses), and the **prefrontal cortex** (involved in regulating emotions and planning). These changes directly affect consciousness, shaping the way a person experiences and interprets their experiences.

However, neuroplasticity also offers hope for recovery. Therapies such as **Exposure Therapy** or **EMDR (Eye Movement Desensitization and Reprocessing)** take advantage of the brain's ability to reorganize itself, helping to "rewrite" automatic responses to trauma and promote new neural connections that allow for a healthier and more balanced perception.

8.5 The Role of Meditation and Mindfulness in Neuroplasticity

One of the most exciting discoveries in the field of neuroplasticity is the impact of **meditation** and **mindfulness** practices on the brain and consciousness. Studies have shown that long-term meditators experience significant changes in brain structures and functions. Regular meditation practice can increase gray matter density in areas of the brain associated with attention, emotional control, and empathy, such as the **anterior cingulate cortex** and **hippocampus**.

The concept of **mindfulness**, which involves focusing intentionally rather than reactively on the present moment, can also lead to decreased activity in the default mode network (DMN), a brain network associated with daydreaming, self-reflection, and ruminating worries. When this network is overactive, it can be associated with feelings of anxiety, depression, and disconnection. Meditation appears to help "train" the brain to decrease rumination and increase focused attention and emotional well-being.

These changes result in a profound modification in conscious experience, allowing for a clearer and more stable state of consciousness. Additionally, meditative practices such as **compassion meditation** (Metta) have been shown to increase empathy and emotional connection, suggesting that neuroplasticity can also be used to cultivate positive qualities of awareness, such as compassion and generosity.

8.6 The Reorganization of the Brain During Rehabilitation

Neuroplasticity has been a key factor in the development of treatments for brain injuries such as strokes, head trauma, or neurodegenerative diseases. When one area of the brain is damaged, other areas can be recruited to take over the lost functions, a process that is encouraged by **rehabilitation therapies** that aim to stimulate these reorganization abilities.

Patients who have suffered a stroke, for example, may lose the ability to speak or move certain parts of the body, but with intensive rehabilitation, many are able to regain these functions. The brain, by reorganizing its connections, can "learn" new ways to perform tasks that were previously performed by the damaged area.

The application of neuroplasticity in rehabilitation is not only physical, but also **cognitive** and **emotional**. Therapies focused on enhancing memory, attention, and emotional control take advantage of the brain's plasticity to reconstruct important aspects of consciousness that have been affected by injury.

8.7 Ethical and Future Implications of Neuroplasticity

Neuroplasticity also raises important ethical questions. As we better understand how the brain can be shaped, possibilities for intervention arise that go beyond rehabilitation and the treatment of diseases. For example, the use of technologies that directly influence neuroplasticity, such as **transcranial magnetic stimulation (TMS)** or **transcranial electrical stimulation**, may open doors to artificial cognitive enhancement.

These technologies can be used to improve memory, creativity, or the ability to focus in healthy individuals, raising questions about the ethical limits of these interventions. What would be the impact of such enhancements on human consciousness? Should we allow the indiscriminate use of technologies that can shape the brain in ways we don't yet fully understand?

In addition, the findings on neuroplasticity also suggest that we are more responsible for our consciousness than we imagined. If the brain can be shaped by our experiences, thoughts, and actions, to what extent are we morally responsible for our own mental and emotional construction?

8.8 The Continual Molding of Consciousness

Neuroplasticity offers us a fascinating insight into consciousness as a dynamic and ever-evolving process. Our experiences, choices, and daily practices have the power to shape our brain and, consequently, our perception and understanding of the world. This means that consciousness, far from being a fixed phenomenon, is a process that can be continuously sculpted.

Chapter 9: The Unconscious: The Hidden Part of Consciousness

Human consciousness, as discussed so far, is only one part of the total functioning of the mind. Behind what we consciously perceive and experience, there is a vast array of mental and emotional processes that occur without our being aware of them—the **unconscious**. From the advent of psychoanalysis with Sigmund Freud, to the more modern theories of cognitive psychology and neuroscience, the unconscious has been one of the most intriguing and fundamental aspects of the study of the human mind. In this chapter, we will explore what the unconscious is, how it has been conceived over time, and how it shapes our perception, behavior, and sense of self.

9.1 Freud and the Unconscious: First Concepts

The concept of the **unconscious** became central to psychology from the theories of **Sigmund Freud**, the father of **psychoanalysis**. For Freud, the human mind was divided into three main parts: the **id**, the **ego,** and the **superego**. Among these, the id represents the deepest, most unconscious part, governed by primal impulses and instinctual desires, such as sex, aggression, and basic needs. The ego, in turn, operates largely in consciousness, regulating and mediating the desires of the id in a way that is compatible with reality and social norms. The superego is the part of the mind that embodies internalized moral and ethical standards.

Freud believed that the unconscious was the reservoir of repressed desires, painful memories, and unresolved conflicts. Much of this content, being socially or morally unacceptable, was kept out of consciousness, but still influenced behavior and emotions. Repression was the mechanism by which these contents were pushed into the unconscious, protecting the individual from conscious anxieties, but creating internal conflicts that manifested themselves indirectly—as in dreams, lapses of the tongue, and neurotic symptoms.

For Freud, the unconscious was not directly accessible, but could be explored through methods such as **free association** and dream **interpretation**. He considered dreams a "royal way" to the unconscious, where repressed desires manifested themselves symbolically.

9.2 Carl Jung and the Collective Unconscious

While Freud emphasized the personal unconscious and its repressed contents, his former disciple **Carl Jung** broadened the idea to include a **collective unconscious**. Jung believed that beyond the individual unconscious, we share a storehouse of memories, symbols, and experiences common to all humanity. This collective unconscious is composed of **archetypes**, which are primordial patterns of behavior and thought present in all cultures and times.

Jungian archetypes **include figures such as the** hero, the shadow **(repressed or rejected aspects of ourselves), the** anima/animus **(internal representations of masculine and**

feminine energies), and the self (the symbol of wholeness and integration). For Jung, the collective unconscious plays a vital role in shaping consciousness, influencing our dreams, mythologies, and behaviors in ways that transcend the individual level.

Jung also introduced the concept of **individuation**, the process by which an individual becomes aware of their unconscious and integrates its repressed or unknown aspects. This process is seen as essential for complete psychological development, allowing the individual to achieve a more balanced and authentic state of existence.

9.3 The Unconscious in Modern Cognitive Psychology

Although the Freudian concept of the unconscious has been criticized and revised over time, the idea that much of mental processing occurs outside of consciousness is widely accepted today, especially in the field of **cognitive psychology** and **neuroscience.**

In cognitive psychology, the unconscious is seen as a set of automatic mental processes that influence behavior without the need for conscious introspection. Processes such as perception, memory, and decision-making can be influenced by information that does not reach the level of consciousness, but that profoundly shapes how we interpret the world.

A classic example of these unconscious processes is **priming**, where exposure to a stimulus, such as a word or image, influences our response to a subsequent stimulus, even if we are unaware of that influence. Another example is **heuristics**, or mental shortcuts that we use to make decisions quickly and efficiently, often without being aware of them.

Studies on **implicit bias** also reveal how the unconscious can influence our perceptions and social behaviors. Implicit biases are biases or preferences that operate below the level of consciousness and can affect decisions in contexts such as hiring employees or legal judgments, even when the person believes they are acting fairly and impartially.

9.4 The Emotional Unconscious

In addition to unconscious cognitive processes, the field of emotional psychology also highlights the existence of an **emotional unconscious**, where feelings and emotional reactions are processed outside of consciousness. Neuroscientist **Antonio Damasio** argues that emotions play a crucial role in decision-making and conscious behavior, but they are often activated by stimuli and contexts automatically and unconsciously.

For example, we may feel aversion or discomfort towards someone without knowing exactly why. This unconscious emotional response may be the result of associations that are not accessible to the conscious mind, but that shape our behavior. The ability to react emotionally to situations quickly and automatically has an adaptive function, allowing us to respond to dangers or opportunities before we even have time to consciously process them.

Emotional intelligence can be seen as the ability to recognize and work with these unconscious processes, developing a greater awareness of how our emotions influence our thoughts and behaviors. Techniques such as **psychotherapy** and **mindfulness** are often used to bring these unconscious reactions to consciousness, allowing for a more informed and less reactive response.

9.5 Neuroscience and the Unconscious: The Role of Automatic Processes

With the advancement of neuroimaging technologies, scientists have been able to map how unconscious processes operate in the brain. Much of the brain's activity occurs outside of conscious awareness, and specific areas are involved in the automatic processing of information.

The **amygdala**, for example, is a key structure in emotional processing, especially related to fear and the fight-or-flight response. When a threatening stimulus is perceived, the amygdala can trigger a rapid response before the conscious cortex has even had time to interpret the danger. This is what allows us to react instantly to a snake on the ground by jumping backwards before we have time to think rationally about what we are seeing.

Another example of unconscious processes at work is **subliminal perception**. In studies, people exposed to images or words for such brief periods of time that they are not consciously perceived still show changes in their behaviors and preferences. These findings show that the brain is able to process information at levels below conscious awareness, and that this information can influence decisions and emotions.

9.6 Dreams: The Theater of the Unconscious

Dreams are traditionally seen as one of the most direct channels of access to the unconscious. For Freud, dreams were an expression of repressed desires, often of a sexual or aggressive nature, that could not be expressed directly in conscious life. However, instead of being presented literally, the wishes in the dream appeared in a distorted or symbolic way, requiring interpretation.

Carl Jung, in turn, saw dreams as a form of communication between the unconscious and the conscious, revealing not only repressed desires, but also aspects of the psyche that needed to be integrated into the conscious personality. For Jung, dreams offered an opportunity for psychological growth, helping the dreamer become more aware of their deepest self.

In the field of neuroscience, dreams are often studied in the context of REM (Rapid Eye Movement) sleep, a phase of sleep characterized by intense brain activity. While the exact function of dreams is still the subject of debate, many researchers believe they play a role in memory processing and emotional regulation, with the brain organizing and integrating experiences in an unconscious way.

9.7 The Unconscious and Creativity

Creativity is another area where the unconscious plays a crucial role. Many artists, writers, and scientists report that their most innovative ideas arise spontaneously, as if they came from a place beyond the conscious mind. This is in line with the view that the unconscious is a source of innovation and originality.

According to Freud, creativity was a sublimation of unconscious impulses—a way of channeling repressed desires into socially acceptable forms such as art and literature. For Jung, creativity was an expression of the archetypes of the collective unconscious, allowing the individual psyche to connect with universal themes of human experience.

Modern psychology also explores the role of the unconscious in the **incubation of ideas**. "Incubation" refers to the period when the mind, seemingly detached from a problem, continues to work on it unconsciously, until a solution or insight suddenly emerges. This process is often mentioned in the field of **creative problem-solving**, where letting the mind "rest" or changing focus can make it easier to generate ideas.

9.8 Exploring the Unconscious: Techniques and Therapies

The study and exploration of the unconscious still play a central role in many psychotherapeutic approaches. In addition to Freudian psychoanalysis, which uses dream interpretation and free association to reveal the unconscious, other therapeutic approaches have developed with the aim of accessing these hidden contents.

Hypnotherapy, for example, is a technique that attempts to access the unconscious in a more direct way, inducing a state of deep relaxation where automatic patterns of thought and behavior can be more easily influenced.

Another example is **Cognitive-Behavioral Therapy (CBT)**, which, although focused on more conscious processes, recognizes the influence of automatic and unconscious patterns on thoughts and behaviors. CBT helps patients identify and modify these patterns to promote positive changes in behavior and perception.

Chapter 10: Consciousness in Altered States

Human consciousness is, in its ordinary form, a stable and continuous process. However, this stability can be interrupted and modified by several factors, creating what we call **altered states of consciousness**. These states can occur naturally or induced, through practices such as meditation, use of psychoactive substances, near-death experiences, hypnosis, and even through extreme activities, such as sleep deprivation or prolonged fasting.

In this chapter, we will explore how consciousness can be modified, the scientific and psychological theories that explain these phenomena, and the impact these states have on our understanding of reality, the mind, and the self.

10.1 What Are Altered States of Consciousness?

Altered states of consciousness (EAC) refer to any condition in which the normal experience of consciousness is significantly different from the standard waking state. This can include changes in sensory perception, time perception, thinking, emotions, and self-awareness. These states can be temporary, such as in a trance or during a deep meditation session, or more prolonged, as in some forms of psychosis or under the influence of psychoactive substances.

Charles Tart, one of the pioneers in the study of CAEs, described these states as experiences that differ qualitatively from waking consciousness, but that can be equally internally coherent. That is, although the content of these experiences is different, within the altered state, there is a logic and coherence that can be understood and explored scientifically.

10.2 Meditation and Expanded Awareness

Meditation is one of the oldest and most widely studied ways of inducing altered states of consciousness. Cultures around the world, especially in Eastern traditions such as **Buddhism** and Hinduism, have for centuries practiced forms of meditation to achieve heightened or expanded states of consciousness. The practice of meditation can alter one's perception of time, increase sensory awareness, and foster a deep sense of connection to one's self and one's surroundings.

Neuroscientists who study meditation have found measurable changes in brain activity during these states. Deep meditation, especially forms such as transcendental meditation and mindfulness, is associated with increased activity in the frontal areas of the brain, which are linked to attention and emotional regulation. In addition, experienced meditation practitioners show changes in brain waves, with an increase in the production of **alpha waves** and **theta waves**, which are associated with states of relaxation and internal attention.

A fascinating discovery is the phenomenon known as **ego boundary-losing**. During deep states of meditation, many practitioners report a sense of merging with the universe or a loss of distinction between the self and the outside world. This experience is interpreted in a variety of ways, from a spiritual connection to a greater reality to a temporary dissolution of the ego's mental constructs.

10.3 Hypnosis: The Control of Consciousness

Hypnosis is another widely used technique to alter consciousness, allowing individuals to access memories and sensations that are normally out of reach of the conscious mind. During a hypnotic state, the individual becomes highly suggestible, and is able to respond to commands or suggestions in a more direct and immediate manner. Hypnosis is often used as a therapeutic tool to treat problems such as chronic pain, anxiety, addictions, and post-traumatic stress disorders.

Scientifically, hypnosis is understood as a state of intense concentration and selective focus, which can be compared to trance or flow states. Neuroimaging studies show that during hypnosis, there is a decrease in activity in the **dorsolateral prefrontal cortex**, an area of the brain involved in critical thinking and self-awareness. This may explain why hypnotized individuals are more likely to accept suggestions without the interference of critical judgments.

In addition, the **anterior cingulate cortex**, which is involved in controlling attention, shows increased activity, which suggests that hypnosis allows for intense focus on a specific task or cue, while also "disabling" other conscious processes. These findings reinforce the idea that hypnosis is a unique state of consciousness, which can be exploited both for therapeutic purposes and for understanding how the brain regulates conscious experience.

10.4 Psychoactive Substances and Expansion of Consciousness

The use of **psychoactive substances** to alter consciousness has a long history, both in ritualistic and recreational contexts. Drugs such as **psilocybin** (found in certain mushrooms), **LSD,** and **DMT** are known to induce powerful altered states of consciousness, which can include intense visual experiences, altered perception of time and space, and a deep sense of transcendence or oneness with the universe.

Psychedelic substances have been used by indigenous cultures in ceremonial contexts for millennia. Recently, scientists have renewed interest in the use of these substances in the treatment of mental illnesses such as depression, anxiety and post-traumatic stress disorder (PTSD). Studies with **psilocybin**, for example, have shown that it can help significantly reduce symptoms of treatment-resistant depression, as well as induce experiences of "expanded awareness" that lead to lasting change in the patient's perspective.

From a neuroscientific point of view, these substances seem to act by promoting the **temporary disintegration of control networks** in the brain. The **prefrontal cortex**, which regulates behavior and conscious thought, loses some of its influence over other areas of the brain, allowing sensory and emotional information to flow more freely. This can result in experiences that are interpreted as deeply meaningful, spiritual, or even mystical, depending on the context and the individual.

10.5 Near-Death Experiences: The Frontier of Consciousness

Near-death experiences (NDEs) are another widely studied phenomenon in the field of altered states of consciousness. Individuals who go through these experiences often report sensations of floating out of their bodies, visions of intense light, encounters with deceased loved ones or beings, and a sense of deep peace. While there are many spiritual or religious interpretations for these experiences, scientists try to understand them from a neurobiological perspective.

A common theory is that NDEs are caused by changes in oxygen levels in the brain, particularly during extreme trauma such as cardiac arrest or hemorrhage. As the brain enters a state of lack of oxygenation (hypoxia), activity in areas such as the **temporal lobe** and **visual cortex** is altered, which could explain the reported sights and sensations. However, the subjective nature of these experiences and the difficulty of studying them in the laboratory mean that they remain one of the greatest mysteries of human consciousness.

Interestingly, many people who experience NDEs report a profound psychological transformation after the event, including a greater appreciation of life, less fear of death, and a shift in personal priorities. These changes suggest that, regardless of the biological cause, NDEs can induce an altered state of consciousness that has a profound and lasting impact on the individual's sense of self and reality.

10.6 Flow: The Ideal State of Consciousness

The concept of **flow** was popularized by psychologist **Mihaly Csikszentmihalyi** as a state in which a person is completely immersed in an activity, feeling a sense of focus, involvement, and intrinsic pleasure. This state is characterized by a loss of sense of time, a balance between challenge and skill, and a fusion between action and awareness, where the person "forgets" about themselves and everything around them, except for the task at hand.

The flow has been studied in several areas, from sports and the arts to the work environment. When a person is in a state of flow, the brain seems to function more efficiently, with optimal synchronization between different brain areas. The **prefrontal cortex**, normally associated with critical thinking and self-awareness, experiences a temporary decrease in activity, which allows for more intuitive and spontaneous focus.

This altered state of consciousness is often associated with optimal performance as well as a sense of deep satisfaction. The search for the flow state can be seen as a way to achieve a balance between the conscious and unconscious mind, where control and freedom coexist in a harmonious way.

10.7 Sensory Deprivation and Sleep Deprivation

Sensory **deprivation** and **sleep deprivation** are extreme methods of inducing altered states of consciousness. When the brain is deprived of external stimuli or the opportunity for rest, it begins to generate its own activity, which can result in visual and auditory hallucinations and feelings of dissociation.

Flotation **tanks** are an example of how sensory deprivation can induce altered states. In these tanks, individuals float in water with a high concentration of salt, without external stimuli such as light or sound. After a certain period, many report feelings of transcendence, merging with the environment, or visionary experiences.

Sleep deprivation, in turn, can induce a gradual disintegration of normal consciousness. As the brain becomes more exhausted, it begins to have difficulties differentiating between wakefulness and dreaming, leading to hallucinatory experiences and perceptual distortions. This altered state, though dangerous if prolonged, reveals the dramatic ways in which the human mind responds to lack of sleep, entering territories where the line between objective and subjective reality becomes blurred.

Chapter 11: Conscience and Free Will

The question of **free will** has fascinated philosophers, psychologists, and neuroscientists for centuries. It challenges us to reflect on one of the most fundamental questions of existence: are we really the agents of our own actions or are we subject to unconscious, biological and deterministic forces? In this chapter, we will explore the relationship between consciousness and free will, discussing different philosophical theories and scientific findings that have challenged our understanding of the extent to which our decisions are conscious and free.

11.1 The Concept of Free Will Throughout History

The concept of **free will** has been rooted in philosophy since Ancient Greece, with philosophers such as **Socrates**, **Plato**, and **Aristotle** discussing the ability of human beings to freely choose between different options. Later, religious traditions also incorporated this notion, suggesting that the ability to freely choose is what makes humans morally responsible for their actions. In the Christian tradition, for example, free will is essential to the idea of sin and redemption.

However, as science progressed, especially with the revolution in **Newtonian physics**, the idea arose that the universe could be a deterministic system, where all actions and events are the result of previous causes. This called into question freedom of choice, leading philosophers to debate whether free will could actually exist in a universe governed by immutable physical laws.

11.2 Biological Determinism: The Limitations of Choice

With advances in biology and neuroscience, theories have emerged that suggest that our behavior may be largely governed by factors that are beyond conscious control. The concept of **biological determinism** states that genes, brain structure, and even levels of neurochemicals can strongly influence our choices and actions. Researchers have shown that conscious decisions are often preceded by unconscious brain activity, challenging the notion that we fully control our actions.

A remarkable experiment in this field is that of **Benjamin Libet**, in the 1980s, who examined the moment when a person decides to perform an action in relation to the moment when the brain begins to prepare for that action. Libet found that there is a "readiness potential" in the brain that occurs about 300 milliseconds before the person is aware of the decision to act. This raised the idea that the brain has already "decided" before the person becomes aware of that decision, suggesting that free will may be an illusion.

However, Libet himself introduced the idea of a "conscious veto"—the possibility that, although the brain initiates actions unconsciously, consciousness may still have the ability to interfere and prevent the execution of an action. This model suggests that even if full free will is questionable, we can still exert some level of control over our actions.

11.3 The Neuroscience of Free Will

Modern neuroscience continues to investigate the relationship between consciousness and free will. The development of technologies such as **functional magnetic resonance imaging (fMRI)** has allowed scientists to observe in real time the regions of the brain that are activated during decision-making. This research suggests that different parts of the brain contribute to different types of decisions:

the **prefrontal cortex** appears to be involved in more rational and planned decisions, while the **limbic system** and **nucleus accumbens** are linked to more emotional and impulsive decisions.

In addition, studies show that the environment, both physical and social, exerts a great influence on our choices, often without us being aware of it. The theory of **priming effects** shows how exposure to certain stimuli can influence a person's behavior without them realizing it. For example, seeing images of money can make a person more likely to make selfish decisions, or listening to a certain song can affect a consumer's purchase choice.

These findings raise questions about the extent to which our decisions are truly free. If our brains are constantly being influenced by unconscious processes and environmental factors, does that mean that free will is just an illusion generated by consciousness?

11.4 Free Will and Moral Responsibility

Despite evidence suggesting that many of our decisions are influenced by unconscious processes, the concept of **moral responsibility** continues to be central to social and legal organization. The belief that we are responsible for our actions forms the basis of the justice system, where it is assumed that individuals can be judged for their choices.

Philosopher **Daniel Dennett** advocates a compatibilist view of free will, which suggests that biological determinism and moral responsibility can coexist. For Dennett, free will does not depend on absolute freedom, but on a capacity for reasoning and reflection that allows individuals to act in accordance with their values and desires, even if these desires are ultimately determined by biological processes and previous experiences.

In this sense, compatibilist free will recognizes that we are not totally free in our choices, but neither are we completely bound by unconscious forces. The ability to reflect on our actions, ponder alternatives, and adjust our behavior according to goals and principles is what distinguishes the human experience from agency.

11.5 Free Will in Psychology: Self-Control and Freedom of Choice

In the field of psychology, the study of free will is closely linked to the notion of self-control. Self-control refers to the ability to regulate impulses and behaviors in order to achieve long-term goals. Research on the phenomenon of self-control suggests that while we may not have absolute control over our desires or impulses, we can learn to regulate them through mindful practices.

Roy Baumeister, a prominent psychologist, introduced the concept of "willpower" as a limited resource that can be depleted but also strengthened over time. Their studies show that individuals who practice self-control more regularly tend to be more successful in a variety of areas of life, which suggests that free will can be exercised through discipline and self-management.

Another field of psychology, called **choice psychology**, explores how people make decisions and the difficulties that arise with the multitude of options. **Barry Schwartz**, in his book *The Paradox of Choice*, argues that more choices don't always lead to more freedom; in fact, too many choices can create anxiety and paralysis, making it difficult to make decisions. Thus, modern psychology suggests that freedom of choice, while valuable, must be balanced with an understanding of limitations and influences on our decisions.

11.6 The Future of Free Will: Ethical and Technological Implications

As science advances, particularly in areas such as artificial intelligence and neuroscience, new ethical questions emerge regarding free will and autonomy. The creation of **neurotechnologies**, such as devices that can directly influence brain activity, raises the possibility of modifying or even controlling decision-making processes. This leads us to ask: to what extent can free will be preserved in a world where technology has the power to intervene directly in our consciousness?

In addition, **genetic determinism** also presents ethical dilemmas. If our genes influence our behavioral predispositions, how should we treat moral responsibility? Would it be fair to judge or punish someone for actions that may be partially influenced by their genetic makeup?

The study of consciousness and free will continues to be a challenging and fascinating frontier. While evidence suggests that much of our decisions are influenced by unconscious processes, the debate about the degree of conscious control we actually have over our actions is still far from settled.

Chapter 12: The Future of Consciousness

As science and technology advance, the study of **consciousness** enters uncharted territory. New discoveries in **neuroscience**, the development of **artificial intelligence (AI),** and philosophical explorations into the concept of mind suggest that the future of consciousness will be shaped by both technological innovations and changes in our understanding of the human brain. This chapter explores the emerging frontiers of consciousness research, raising fascinating and challenging questions about what it means to be conscious and how these discoveries can transform humanity.

12.1 The Artificial Consciousness Project

One of the most intriguing questions that has arisen with the advancement of digital technologies and AI is whether these machines can one day develop **consciousness**. Today's AI already outperforms humans at certain tasks, such as recognizing patterns in large volumes of data, making quick decisions, and processing complex information. However, even the most advanced AIs, such as neural networks and deep learning algorithms, are still far from showing signs of consciousness in the human sense.

The challenge of creating conscious AI involves not only increasing computational capacity, but also deeply understanding what it takes for something to "feel" or "experience" reality in a subjective way. **David Chalmers**, a renowned philosopher in the field of mind, introduced the idea of the "**hard problem of consciousness**"—the question of how and why certain brain processes produce conscious experiences while others do not. He suggests that even if we can create AI that simulates human behavior perfectly, the internal expertise of these machines could be non-existent.

On the other hand, some scientists and engineers believe that as we better understand the mechanisms that generate consciousness in the human brain, we will be able to replicate them in machines. This raises the possibility of a future in which artificial sentient beings can exist, bringing up deep ethical and philosophical questions. If an AI developed consciousness, would it have rights? Would you be able to feel pain, have desires, or experience the world subjectively like human beings?

12.2 Neuroscience and Brain-Computer Interfaces

Another promising field is that of **brain-computer interfaces (CCI),** which are transforming the way scientists interact with the human mind and consciousness. These technologies allow direct communication between the human brain and external devices, such as computers and robotic prosthetics. At the most basic level, CCIs are already used to help people with motor disabilities control devices with their thoughts, paving the way for more sophisticated forms of mind-machine interaction.

Over time, the development of more advanced CCIs may allow human consciousness to be "expanded" or "merged" with digital systems. Companies like **Neuralink**, founded by **Elon Musk**, are working to develop technologies that could one day allow humans to store memories digitally, or even "transfer" aspects of consciousness to machines. While this idea is still far from being realized, it raises fascinating questions about the nature of the mind. If a person's consciousness could be transferred to an artificial system, would that person still be "himself"? Is human identity inseparable from the biological body, or could it be preserved in another type of substrate?

12.3 Collective Consciousness: The Future of Interconnectedness

With the growth of global connectivity and the expansion of social networks, some theorists suggest that we are moving toward a kind of **collective consciousness**. While this idea has roots in philosophical and spiritual traditions, such as philosopher **Pierre Teilhard de Chardin**'s concept of the **"noosphere,"** modern technology could turn this vision into reality in unexpected ways.

Digital platforms already allow large groups of people to collaborate and share information in real time, creating a continuous flow of data and knowledge. However, the true potential of a collective consciousness could emerge if direct brain communication technologies became viable. Imagine a future where human minds are directly connected, sharing thoughts and emotions on a fundamental level. This could transform society and individuality in profound ways, perhaps even questioning the boundaries between the "I" and the "we."

The ethical challenges of such interconnectedness are vast. What would happen to privacy and the sense of individual identity? Would it be possible to maintain personal autonomy in a world where thoughts could be shared directly between minds? Collective consciousness can bring both benefits and challenges, and the balance between interconnectedness and individuality will be a central theme for the future of humanity.

12.4 Expansion of Human Consciousness

As technology advances, the idea of **expanding human consciousness** goes beyond interconnection with machines or other humans. Many futurists and neuroscientists are exploring ways to augment or enhance the very capacity of the human mind. This can include not only cognitive improvements, such as increased memory or information processing speed, but also more profound changes in the conscious state.

The use of psychoactive substances such as **psilocybin** and **LSD** in therapeutic and self-improvement contexts has once again become the focus of scientific research. Such substances have shown potential to alter the perception of reality and improve creativity and introspection. By combining these approaches with technological advances, such as brain-computer interfaces and artificial intelligence, some researchers believe that we may be able to develop new forms of **augmented consciousness**.

Others, such as transhumanists, argue that the future of humanity includes the **fusion of the human with technology**, creating hybrid beings capable of transcending biological limitations. For these thinkers, the expansion of consciousness is an inevitable path for human evolution.

They argue that by pushing the boundaries of the biological brain, we could reach new levels of self-awareness, intelligence, and understanding of the universe.

12.5 Digital Immortality: The Dream of Preserving Consciousness

One of the greatest challenges in the search for the future of consciousness is the issue of **mortality**. Human consciousness, as currently understood, is inextricably linked to biological life. However, some theorists speculate that we could achieve some level of **digital immortality**.

The idea of transferring consciousness to a digital medium — what is sometimes called **mind uploading** — has been explored in both science fiction and serious philosophical discussions. This concept involves copying or simulating the content of the human mind on a digital platform, which would theoretically allow a version of an individual to continue to exist indefinitely, even after physical death.

However, many questions remain unanswered. Even if it were technically possible to copy all of a person's neural connections and mental content, would that amount to creating a conscious copy? Or was it just a simulation, devoid of real subjective experience? Continuity **of consciousness**, i.e., the experience of existing over time, is essential to personal identity, and this aspect can be lost in a digital upload.

In addition, digital immortality raises significant ethical questions. Who would have access to this technology? How would we deal with the social inequalities that can arise in a world where some can "live" indefinitely, while others remain limited by biology?

12.6 Consciousness Beyond Humanity: The Search for Conscious Life in the Cosmos

As we expand our understanding of consciousness on Earth, another frontier of knowledge is the possibility of **conscious life outside of the planet**. The search for **extraterrestrial intelligence** (SETI) raises fascinating questions about the nature of consciousness in other biological contexts, or even in life forms based on different physical or chemical principles.

If we ever find intelligent life on another planet, one of the central questions will be: how do these life forms experience consciousness? Are we dealing with a mind that shares elements of our subjective experience, or is it something completely alien and incomprehensible to us? The search for conscious life in the cosmos is not only a scientific question, but also a philosophical and existential one, as we strive to understand our place in the universe.

Chapter 13: Consciousness and Spirituality in the Twenty-First Century

Throughout history, consciousness has often been seen as the point of intersection between science and spirituality. In the twenty-first century, renewed interest in the connection between these two fields is growing, as researchers and practitioners try to understand how spiritual experiences and heightened states of consciousness relate to the brain, mind, and universe. This chapter explores how ancient spiritual traditions are being revisited in the light of modern science, and how consciousness continues to be a fertile ground for reflections on the meaning of life, transcendence, and human potential.

13.1 Spirituality and Neuroscience: The Science of Mystical Experience

Many accounts of spiritual experiences involve altered states of consciousness that transcend the individual "self," providing a sense of oneness with the cosmos, the divine, or the natural world. Neuroscience, by studying these experiences, seeks to identify the brain processes involved in mystical or spiritual states. Through techniques such as **functional magnetic resonance imaging (fMRI) and electroencephalography (EEG),** researchers have begun to unravel what happens in the brain during these experiments.

One of the most fascinating fields of study is that of **peak experiences**, described by **Abraham Maslow**. These experiences often involve intense feelings of ecstasy, deep understanding, and a sense of connection to something greater than self. Spiritual practices such as meditation, prayer, and rituals can induce these states, and scientific studies have shown that during these practices, there is a decrease in activity in the **parietal lobe**, which is responsible for spatial orientation, which can contribute to the feeling of "oneness" with the universe, as the boundary between "self" and "other" seems to disappear.

Additionally, there is growing interest in using **psychedelics**, such as **psilocybin** and **DMT**, in therapeutic contexts to elicit mystical experiences that promote emotional healing and self-knowledge. Pioneering research at universities such as **Johns Hopkins** demonstrates that, in controlled environments, these substances can help people overcome deep trauma, cope with anxiety, and reconnect with a spiritual meaning in life. These findings are challenging traditional preconceptions about psychedelic drugs and opening up a new field of study on the relationship between consciousness and the spiritual.

13.2 The Expansive Mind: Awareness and Contemplative Practices

Contemplative practices **such as** meditation **and** mindfulness have gained popularity in the twenty-first century, not only for their mental health benefits but also for their ability to expand consciousness. Thousands of studies show that these practices can alter the structure and function of the brain, promoting a state of presence, self-awareness, and emotional balance. Through regular practice, many report a growing sense of interconnectedness, both with other humans and with the natural world, which resonates deeply with many spiritual traditions.

Meditation, in particular, has been studied for its impact on the **prefrontal cortex**, an area associated with decision-making, self-control, and planning. As people develop greater awareness of their thoughts and emotions, they may also become more aware of their interactions with the world around them. This leads to the concept of **compassionate awareness**, a central idea in traditions such as Buddhism, which emphasizes the interdependence of all forms of life.

In addition, studies on advanced meditation practitioners, such as Tibetan monks, reveal that long periods of practice can lead to significant brain changes, including increased **gray matter** in areas linked to attention and empathy. This suggests that the human mind is capable of an extraordinary level of plasticity, and that the expansion of consciousness can be a gradual process, cultivated over years of deliberate practice.

13.3 Cosmic Consciousness: Philosophical and Spiritual Reflections

The concept of **cosmic consciousness**, proposed by thinkers such as **Richard Maurice Bucke** in the early twentieth century, refers to a state of consciousness that transcends the individual ego and realizes the fundamental unity of the universe. This state of enlightenment, described by many mystics and sages throughout history, is often associated with a deep understanding that the separation between the self and the universe is an illusion.

For many contemporary philosophers, such as **Ken Wilber**, the development of human consciousness occurs in stages, from more basic and egoic levels to levels of spiritual or "transpersonal" consciousness. Wilber describes this process as an **evolution of consciousness**, where the human being gradually moves beyond identification with the individual ego to a more comprehensive understanding of reality.

This idea of cosmic consciousness also connects to the **holistic theory** of the universe, which suggests that the cosmos is an interconnected system, in which consciousness plays a key role. According to this view, consciousness is not just a byproduct of the brain, but an essential aspect of reality that permeates all things. In other words, our own mind can be seen as an individualized manifestation of a universal consciousness.

13.4 Death and Consciousness: The Mystery of the Beyond

One of the oldest and most deeply spiritual questions about consciousness is what happens to it after **death**. Many spiritual traditions believe that consciousness continues to exist in some form, either through reincarnation, as in Hinduism and Buddhism, or in the afterlife, as in the Abrahamic traditions. Modern science, however, faces major challenges when trying to empirically study what happens to consciousness after the death of the body.

One field that is being explored with greater intensity is that of **near-death experiences (NDEs),** which are reports of people who have been clinically declared dead for short periods and, after being resuscitated, have reported having lucid experiences, such as seeing bright lights, feeling a loving presence, or revisiting important moments in their lives. These reports, while still controversial, suggest that consciousness may not be entirely dependent on the biological body.

Researchers like **Sam Parnia**, an expert on NDEs, investigate these experiences using rigorous methods to try to identify whether these phenomena are purely biological—the result of neurological processes when the brain is under stress—or if there is something deeper involved. The possibility that consciousness can transcend the physical body raises questions about the nature of the mind and the intersection between science and spirituality.

13.5 Spirituality in the Digital Age

Technological advancement is transforming all areas of human life, and **spirituality** is no exception. Spiritual practices are adapting to the digital world in ways that would have been unthinkable just a few decades ago. Meditation and mindfulness groups now hold meetups on virtual platforms, and **meditation apps** like **Headspace** and **Calm** reach millions of users, offering spiritual and wellness practices at the touch of a button.

In addition, technology is enabling new ways to explore states of consciousness through **virtual reality (VR)** and **augmented reality (AR).** For example, VR experiences are used to simulate deep meditative states, and digitally created immersive environments can transport participants to "virtual temples" or cosmic landscapes, allowing them to explore their spirituality in new ways.

On the other hand, the increasing reliance on technology raises questions about how to maintain an authentic and centered spirituality amidst constant digital distraction. The balance between the use of technological tools for spiritual growth and the risk of losing touch with the depth of practice will be an ongoing challenge for those seeking a spiritual life in the twenty-first century.

13.6 The Search for Meaning: Consciousness and Purpose in the Twenty-First Century

In an increasingly fast-paced and technological world, many people are searching for a **deeper purpose** and **meaning** for their lives. The relationship between consciousness and spirituality is central to this search. Philosopher and neuroscientist **Sam Harris** argues that while we may live in a universe seemingly devoid of cosmic purpose, the pursuit of heightened states of consciousness and the cultivation of mindfulness can provide us with deep personal meaning, helping us to live more meaningfully.

This modern view of spirituality, which often aligns with a **secular spirituality**, suggests that the meaning and purpose of life can be found not through religious dogma, but through the conscious practice and cultivation of virtues such as compassion, empathy, and altruism. For many, spirituality in the twenty-first century is an internal journey of discovery rather than an adherence to external religious structures.

Epilogue: The Journey of Self-Awareness and the Path to a Healthier Life and Society

Consciousness is the foundation that sustains not only the individual, but also the society. Throughout the chapters, we explore how psychoanalysis, neuroscience, and modern approaches provide us with different lenses through which to understand this vast and multifaceted human experience. However, what becomes clearer, as we advance in the understanding of the mind, is the urgency of turning to ourselves, of dedicating ourselves to developing **awareness of who we are** and, consequently, creating a healthier, more balanced and compassionate society.

The Importance of Self-Awareness

Developing awareness of ourselves is a process that involves confronting our own limitations, traumas, and internal conflicts. For many, this can be an uncomfortable, sometimes painful, but deeply necessary path. Modern life often pressures us to seek external success, recognition, and material fulfillment, leaving aside introspection and care for our **psychic life**.

Self-knowledge involves recognizing our **unconscious patterns** and how they impact our choices, relationships, and attitudes. Psychoanalysis shows us that we are often driven by internal forces that operate outside of our consciousness, whether it is an unresolved trauma, repressed desires, or defense mechanisms that we develop to protect ourselves from suffering. The process of becoming aware of these forces is liberating, as it allows us **to make more authentic choices**, where we are no longer stuck in automatic and repetitive patterns.

The Fundamental Role of the Therapeutic Process

It is in this context that the **therapeutic process** becomes a fundamental tool. Therapy, whether through psychoanalysis, cognitive-behavioral psychology, or other approaches, offers us a safe space to explore our psyche. Here, we can confront our shadows, look at our fears and vulnerabilities, and, with the support of a professional, restructure our view of ourselves and the world.

The therapist acts as a mirror, helping us to see what is hidden and to make sense of feelings and behaviors that sometimes seem incomprehensible. Over time, the therapeutic process promotes an integration between the **conscious and the unconscious**, allowing us to become more whole. As this balance develops, the individual begins to realize that what previously caused suffering — such as traumas, limitations, or internal conflicts — can be understood and transformed.

Understanding Our Traumas and Limitations

One of the central aspects in the development of self-awareness is the understanding of our **traumas**. Traumas can be large and devastating events, but they can also be small experiences accumulated throughout life that generate a profound emotional impact. These experiences are stored in our unconscious, shaping our thoughts, feelings, and behaviors, often without us realizing it.

Recognizing and treating traumas is essential to prevent them from perpetuating. Unresolved trauma can manifest itself in self-destructive patterns, relationship problems, anxiety, depression, or even physical symptoms. By facing them, we not only interrupt this cycle, but also give ourselves the chance to **grow emotionally**, learning to deal with adversity in a healthier and more resilient way.

Likewise, it is essential to accept that we have **limitations**. Part of the process of self-knowledge is to recognize that we are fallible, imperfect beings, with flaws and frailties. However, this is no reason for discouragement; rather, it is an opportunity to accept ourselves as we are, with compassion. By doing so, we free ourselves from the pressure to be perfect and allow personal growth to occur in a more organic and gentle way.

The Benefits of Consciousness for the Individual and for Society

The development of self-awareness has tangible benefits for individual well-being. People who invest in their mental and emotional health experience an increased quality of life, greater clarity in their choices, and an expanded sense of purpose and fulfillment. They become more resilient, able to deal with challenges in a more balanced way, and are less likely to act impulsively or reactively. Understanding one's feelings and motivations reduces anxiety and promotes inner peace.

In addition, this inner transformation reverberates in interpersonal relationships. Self-aware individuals are more empathetic, understanding, and able to communicate openly and honestly. They have less need to project their insecurities onto others, which results in **healthier and more authentic relationships**. This is particularly important in a world where interpersonal and social conflicts often arise from misunderstandings, unrealistic expectations, or unexpressed tensions.

At the **collective** level, a society composed of more conscious individuals is inevitably healthier and more harmonious. The development of awareness promotes a culture of dialogue, tolerance and respect. Societies that value self-knowledge and emotional well-being are better able to deal with their differences and challenges constructively. Understanding individual and collective traumas allows us to face social challenges in a more compassionate way, preventing violence, prejudice and exclusion from being the predominant responses.

Building a More Conscious Future

What becomes evident is that the development of consciousness is an ongoing journey, both on an individual and societal level. **The therapeutic process** is just one of the tools available, but a powerful one that allows each of us to delve into the depths of our psyche and emerge with a clearer and richer understanding of who we are. By becoming more aware of our own motivations and limitations, we gain the ability to navigate life with more wisdom, balance, and empathy.

If we want to build a **more conscious future**, we must start with ourselves. Investing in our mental health, embracing the process of self-discovery, and committing to the journey of healing and growth are actions that not only benefit ourselves but also create a positive impact on our family, friends, colleagues, and ultimately, the society in which we live.

Consciousness makes us **more human**, in the fullest sense of the word. It gives us the ability to realize our connections with others, to see ourselves as part of something bigger, and to act in a more responsible and compassionate way. By developing this awareness, we are actually planting the seeds for a society where respect, empathy, and mutual understanding are the core values. And so, together, we can walk the path to a more balanced and conscious world.

About the Author

Born in 1992, Michael Sousa is Brazilian and has lived in Lisbon for a few years, holds a master's degree in International Trade from the European Business School in Barcelona, MBA in Strategic Management from FEA-RP USP, a degree in Computer Science and a specialist in Strategic Foresight. He has an extension in Applied Statistics and in Cost Management. He works with Project Management, Data Analysis and Market Intelligence. However, surrendering to his interest in Freudian theories, he also went to study Psychoanalysis at the Brazilian Institute of Clinical Psychoanalysis, and specialized in the subject and in clinical practice. When he doesn't spend his free time trying to develop his lousy artistic side, he finds himself studying the political-economic collapse of nations, psychoanalytic texts, or over many a quaint and curious volume of forgotten lore.

www.ingramcontent.com/pod-product-compliance
Lightning Source LLC
LaVergne TN
LVHW011931070526
838202LV00054B/4588